Alexander
The LONDON
of POLITICS
October

CS

▶ The Entrepreneur in History

DOI: 10.1057/9781137305824

Other Palgrave Pivot titles

DOI: 10.1057/9781137305824

palgrave▶pivot

The Entrepreneur in History: From Medieval Merchant to Modern Business Leader

Mark Casson
Professor of Economics, University of Reading

and

Catherine Casson
Research Fellow, Winton Institute for Monetary History, Ashmolean Museum, University of Oxford and Teaching Fellow, School of History and Cultures, University of Birmingham

palgrave macmillan

DOI: 10.1057/9781137305824

First published 2013 by
PALGRAVE MACMILLAN

Palgrave Macmillan in the UK is an imprint of Macmillan Publishers Limited, registered in England, company number 785998, of Houndmills, Basingstoke, Hampshire RG21 6XS.

Palgrave Macmillan in the US is a division of St Martin's Press LLC, 175 Fifth Avenue, New York, NY 10010.

Palgrave Macmillan is the global academic imprint of the above companies and has companies and representatives throughout the world.

Palgrave® and Macmillan® are registered trademarks in the United States, the United Kingdom, Europe and other countries.

ISBN: 978–1–137–30583–1 EPUB
ISBN: 978–1–137–30582–4 PDF
ISBN: 978–1–137–30581–7 Hardback

A catalogue record for this book is available from the British Library.

A catalog record for this book is available from the Library of Congress.

www.palgrave.com/pivot

DOI: 10.1057/9781137305824

Contents

List of Tables

DOI: 10.1057/9781137305824

Preface and Acknowledgements

This book was written especially for the Palgrave Pivot series. It sets out a new research agenda and reports some key findings. It is intended to be authoritative but also provocative. We are grateful to Virginia Thorp of Palgrave Macmillan for her support and encouragement.

The research for this book involved an extensive review of the literature, which led to the identification of a set of 60 key articles. These articles, together with selected book excerpts, are reprinted in a research collection, *The History of Entrepreneurship: Innovation and Risk-taking, 1200–2000*, which can be studied in conjunction with this book.

Parts of Chapter 2 were presented at a conference organised by the Centre for Entrepreneurship, Henley Business School, University of Reading, 2012; parts of Chapter 3 at the Annual Conference of the Association of Business Historians at Reading, 2011; and parts of Chapter 4 at the Conference on New Business History at the University of York, 2012. Valuable comments were received from discussants in each case.

Some of the material has formed the basis for lectures to undergraduate and postgraduate students in the School of History and Cultures, University of Birmingham and the Henley Business School, University of Reading. We are grateful to the students and to colleagues for their positive feedback and for the suggestions they have made.

Last but not least, we are indebted to Janet Casson for proof-reading the manuscript and for moral support.

palgrave▶**pivot**

www.palgrave.com/pivot

1

A New Research Agenda

Abstract: *Entrepreneurship is of contemporary interest. The self-employed entrepreneur is an aspirational figure and one that many students in particular wish to emulate. Despite this, there is still relatively little study of entrepreneurship in the era before the rise of the modern corporation. The introduction explains how the book is grounded on two principles. Firstly, that the theory of entrepreneurship needs to be presented in a rigorous fashion which explains why it is valuable to the economy. Secondly, that the study of entrepreneurship needs to be examined over a long historical perspective. The introduction then outlines the methodology used in the rest of the book.*

Casson, Mark and Casson, Catherine. *The Entrepreneur in History: From Medieval Merchant to Modern Business Leader.* Basingstoke: Palgrave Macmillan, 2013. DOI: 10.1057/9781137305824.

1.1   Aims of the book

Contemporary enterprise culture promotes the entrepreneur as a role model. The self-employed entrepreneur is an aspirational figure at a time when there are limited vacancies in established firms. For those seeking to start their own business, the image of the entrepreneur is very attractive. The successful entrepreneur personifies the positive qualities of the sort of person they would like to become.

These ambitions are reflected at university. Many students decide that a degree in business studies will be the best route for becoming an entrepreneur. Such a degree offers practical training and the opportunity to cover the cost of rising tuition fees by earnings from future employment.

Entrepreneurship has become part of the business studies curriculum, but it is sometimes taught in a superficial way that relies on popular stereotypes rather than rigorous analysis. The study of business history has become disconnected from the study of entrepreneurship. In entrepreneurship studies the emphasis is usually on the independent judgement of the entrepreneur and their willingness to pursue opportunities overlooked by other people. In business history, by contrast, the emphasis is often on the emergence of the managerial corporation; the intellectual challenge is to explain the emergence of large bureaucratic businesses in the early twentieth century rather than the re-emergence of vibrant small businesses in the late twentieth century. This is not a particularly interesting question for many students today, because they do not aspire to work in such firms. Managers in these large corporations were expected to conform in their thinking and to take decisions using prescribed procedures rather than by exercising their own initiative. This is not an attractive career model for today's students. In contrast, students today would prefer to set up their own business rather than become a 'well-suited' executive in a large firm. They would also rather work in a business that pursues ecologically sound and sustainable objectives rather than one that appears to be dedicated to maximising short-run shareholder value.

Business history is changing, and there is now much more emphasis on small firms, and in particular on clusters of small firms associated with industrial districts. Change comes rather slowly, however. There is still relatively little study of entrepreneurship in the era before the rise of the modern corporation. Where such studies exist

DOI: 10.1057/9781137305824

they generally go back no further than the Industrial Revolution of the eighteenth century, or the financial revolution of the seventeenth century.

This book is based on two principles. The first is that contemporary enterprise culture offers a distorted view of entrepreneurship. The theory of entrepreneurship needs to be presented to students in a more rigorous fashion. It is necessary to explain why entrepreneurship is valuable to the economy. Entrepreneurship is a scarce resource that allows other resources, such as land, labour and capital, to be put to better use. Entrepreneurs provide good judgement that improves the quality of business decision-making. In the absence of entrepreneurship more mistakes would be made: valuable opportunities to innovate would be overlooked, and resources would be wasted instead on superficially attractive projects that ultimately fail.

The second principle is that the study of entrepreneurship needs to be grounded in historical evidence. General theories of entrepreneurship should be tested over the long term, not the short term. It is all very well developing general theories of entrepreneurship, but it is rather pointless to test them using only the evidence of the last 40 years. Business archives often go back for a hundred years or more. Furthermore entrepreneurs often appear in the records of national and local government, which in some European countries go back for 800 years. Although individual scholars have used these early records to study particular individuals, there has been no systematic approach to the use of this evidence. This book therefore outlines a research agenda for the history of entrepreneurship that involves exploiting the full range of evidence, and explains how this agenda can be implemented.

1.2   Summary of the theory

The basic idea behind the economic theory of entrepreneurship is that entrepreneurship is fundamentally the same whenever and wherever it occurs. It does not change because it is a function, and this function is always in demand. It is a capacity to make decisions better than other people. It is exercised by taking responsibility for decisions that other people would find difficult. A typical example is a decision whether or not to invest in a new product or technology when the cost is high and the benefits are uncertain.

DOI: 10.1057/9781137305824

An entrepreneur may acquire the power to make big decisions because they have set up a business in which other people have invested. Other people have invested because they are confident that the entrepreneur can be trusted to make better judgements that they could themselves. This establishes a link between the function of the entrepreneur and the role that they play in society. The entrepreneur is typically the owner or manager of a business, or a partner in it. The business implements the investments that the entrepreneur selects, collects the profits and pays back the investors, leaving a surplus for rewarding the entrepreneur.

The function of the entrepreneur is the same across time and space. Geography affects the kinds of industries to which the function is applied in any particular country, and the kinds of natural hazards (such as extremes of weather) that are encountered. The political system determines how much discretion the entrepreneur possesses to establish their own business, and the level of taxes and regulation to which they are subjected, but it does not affect their basic function. Time is also important; the earlier the date, the lower the level of technology and the greater the costs of transport and trade, but the challenge is still the same: to improve upon the status quo, whatever that may be.

Entrepreneurship is valuable because the resource that it uses is scarce. This resource is the cognitive ability of the entrepreneur. This ability depends on a number of factors. Entrepreneurs must be able to collect and process information quickly and accurately. They are not mere human computers, however. They need social skills in order to acquire information from other people. They need imagination to visualise opportunities that have not yet been exploited and to conceptualise new products that have not yet been developed. They need all of these qualities, and not just some of them, and this makes a good entrepreneur extremely scarce. Good entrepreneurs can earn big rewards because they are sought after by investors. By entrusting their resources to a good entrepreneur investors can avoid the costly mistakes that a not-so-good entrepreneur would be liable to make.

This establishes a link between the function of the entrepreneur, the role they play, and the qualities they require. These qualities are often expressed in terms of personality (as revealed in attitudes) and competences (skills). It is often assumed that a successful entrepreneur is a supremely confident extrovert who loves taking risks. This impression arises from the fact that some entrepreneurs are very good at

DOI: 10.1057/9781137305824

publicising themselves by telling the public what they want to hear; in modern business jargon, an adventurous image reinforces the value of the brand. Close examination of the evidence, however, suggests that many successful entrepreneurs maintain a low profile, and are cautious in the investments they make. Their investments appear risky only because other people do not possess the privileged information that the entrepreneurs use to arrive at their decisions. Given the difficulty of looking inside the head of the entrepreneur, the safest conclusion is that successful entrepreneurs have a well-balanced personality that allows them to cope well in a variety of situations. It is also useful for them to possess self-awareness, so that they can recognise their own limitations and avoid situations with which they cannot cope, or can hire other people who can help them.

Given the function, role, personality and competencies of the entrepreneur, it is possible to deduce how they will behave in different situations. It is impossible to make precise predictions, however, because only the entrepreneur knows the details of the situation in which they are placed, and they cannot always be relied upon to give a truthful account of them later. It is fairly obvious, however, that a successful entrepreneur will tend to have a strategy to combat the most obvious threats to their business and a contingency plan to deal with the most obvious risks. This will allow the entrepreneur to 'keep a level head' under conditions that others may perceive as critical. A successful entrepreneur will 'stay ahead of them game' and out-manoeuvre rivals who are trying to out-manoeuvre them. The links between function, role, personality, competencies, behaviour and performance are summarised in Table 1.1.

Successful entrepreneurs often lead rather different lives from what popular culture suggests. Entrepreneurs have to learn from their mistakes, like everyone else, and their initial business ventures are not always successful. Entrepreneurs who survive in business generally do so by managing risks rather than by deliberately seeking them out. Taking a big risk can generate a spectacular return in the short run, but such a strategy is not really sustainable. Many entrepreneurs who made quick fortunes also lost them just as quickly with their next speculation, and ended their career in poverty or debt. History, however, often records their successes and overlooks their failures, thereby giving a false impression. The problem is compounded by ignoring the unglamorous achievements of low-profile entrepreneurs who successfully managed risk throughout their careers.

DOI: 10.1057/9781137305824

TABLE 1.1   *Different ways in which entrepreneurs have been defined*

Basis of definition	Explanation
Function	Innovation, risk taking, judgement in project selection
Role	Founder of firm, owner-manager, partner, salaried chief executive
Personality (attitudes, skills)	Self-confident: both imaginative and pragmatic Takes a distinctive view of the world
Competence (skills)	Good judgement Seeing the bigger picture (putting the jigsaw together) Looking for the hidden snag Basic business skills (law, accountancy, IT, etc.)
Behaviour	Takes responsibility Makes timely decisions (no procrastination) Motivates (rather than alienates) colleagues
Performance	Success is typically measured by wealth accumulation and reputation, although quality of lifestyle may also be a factor. Success reflects the availability of opportunities, good luck and appropriate personality and competence

1.3   The value of a historical perspective

Studying a subject such as entrepreneurship over a very long period of time is useful because it is possible to see long-term processes at work. It is possible to track the impacts of innovations and to assess how far one innovation spawns another, as shown in Chapter 3. It is also possible to examine how entrepreneurs promoting rival projects resolve their conflicts and to examine the characteristics of the winners.

A difficulty with any long-term study, however, is that the context is continually changing. A person who is called an entrepreneur today may have been called a promoter two centuries ago, and an adventurer before that. An entrepreneur today sets up a firm, but two centuries ago they would probably have set up a partnership instead. Theory suggests that entrepreneurship is fundamentally the same today as it was before, but this is difficult to assess if the context is radically different.

The problem of context becomes even greater if a study is conducted on a global basis, because then the context changes according to the politics and culture of the country concerned. To avoid the complexities of an international study, this book concentrates mainly on a single country,

DOI: 10.1057/9781137305824

namely England. This is a country which is noted for its enterprise in the eighteenth and nineteenth centuries, and is one where business records are particularly good over the long term.

English history is examined though the lens of various revolutions in the economy which historians have described, the earliest of which witnessed the growth of market towns and the most recent of which saw the growing dominance of the modern multinational enterprise. Revolutions can be regarded as the outcome of interrelated innovations, in which entrepreneurship has played a prominent role. Identifying the specific innovations involved in a given revolution is relatively straightforward, but identifying the individual entrepreneurs is not. The attribution of initiative is culture-dependent: entrepreneurs are celebrities at one time and almost invisible at others. Developing a method for identifying entrepreneurs and their historical impacts is one of the tasks of this book.

Where there is a lack of evidence on an historical subject, such as the role of the entrepreneur, it might be expected that scholars would adopt an agnostic position. Far from it: 'nature abhors a vacuum', it is said, and so sweeping generalisations emerge instead. These generalisations are often ideologically based. Left-wingers tend to argue that entrepreneurs are responsible for the inequalities in society because of the enormous profits they make, whilst right-wingers maintain that entrepreneurs are public benefactors because of the innovations they make. Historians of a Marxian persuasion tend to support the first position whilst free-market economic historians espouse the second.

This book espouses neither view. It argues that entrepreneurial innovations are risky, and may succeed or fail. Furthermore, even those that succeed may benefit the entrepreneur much more than they benefit society as a whole. On the other hand, without entrepreneurship there would be less innovation – not only less bad innovation, which might be a benefit, but less good innovation, which would be a cost. If one innovation leads to another, as often claimed, then reducing good innovations will impair the prospect for good innovations in the future too. Bad innovations, on the other hand, do not necessarily lead to other bad innovations, so that increasing the number of bad innovations may have a more limited effect. Each society has to strike a balance between these effects. Different societies will take different attitudes, and this will be reflected in their long-term economic performance. The historical study of entrepreneurship can identify the factors that influence these choices,

DOI: 10.1057/9781137305824

and reveal how different choices made at different times in different countries have led to different outcomes.

1.4   A case study approach

The case study approach has a long and distinguished record in the study of entrepreneurship. The case study method is well-established in the teaching of business and management studies, and the company case study is a well-established feature of traditional business history. The method is applied in Chapter 4 to study the careers of individual entrepreneurs.

Until recently, business history case studies have tended to focus on the firm rather than the individual entrepreneur. In the late 1940s business historians associated with a research centre in entrepreneurial history at Harvard University set out to focus on the individual entrepreneur, but their efforts achieved only limited success. Popular interest at the time centred on the emergence of the modern corporation, as charted by a later generation of Harvard business historians. It was believed that the modern corporation, with its team of professional managers, was not constrained by the competencies of a single individual, as was the traditional entrepreneurial firm, and it was therefore confidently expected that large firms would supersede small firms in the post-war economy, as they did, to some extent, for a short period of time. Business historians therefore dedicated themselves to writing the history of the rise of the modern corporation, in which the enlightened professional manager, rather than the individual entrepreneur, was the heroic figure.

The theory of entrepreneurship suggests, however, that focusing a case study on the firm is a mistake. Firms are usually established by entrepreneurs in order to exploit an opportunity they believe they have discovered. The firm is established after the opportunity has been recognised and not before; it is a nexus of contracts and a hub of communications, set up to exploit the opportunity in a systematic way. The key to understanding the opportunity therefore lies in studying the entrepreneur. The biography of the entrepreneur leads to the investigation of the firm, and not the other way round.

Chapter 4 is based on a survey of the existing case study literature on the history of entrepreneurship. Over 20 case studies are summarised, with the earliest entrepreneurs appearing first. The studies cover a range

DOI: 10.1057/9781137305824

of industries, but not all of them contain biographical information, because such information is very scarce, particularly for early periods. The case studies demonstrate that it is possible to link the behaviour of entrepreneurs to the successes and failures of the firms they create or control. It shows that many successful entrepreneurs fail at some stage, either early in their career, due to inexperience, or later, due to overconfidence. Popular history tends to record their successes. However, some of the most spectacularly successful entrepreneurs also experienced the most spectacular failures, probably as a consequence of taking excessive risk. Taking risks can generate big returns in the short run but big losses in the long run.

1.5   Social and institutional context

Chapter 5 examines the social and institutional context of entrepreneurship. It suggests that successful entrepreneurs possess social skills which enable them to profit from the cultural and political structures in which they operate. In particular they are good at exploiting social networks for business ends.

Chapter 5 also examines the extent to which entrepreneurs can influence the social environment in which they operate. They can do this for either selfish or altruistic reasons, or for a combination of the two. Altruism is characteristic of the social entrepreneur. Social entrepreneurs tend to be mission-driven; they act as leaders by forming clubs, societies, and even political and religious movements. These organisations are typically organised on a non-profit basis. They exploit opportunities for coordination that a conventional business cannot exploit. Unlike charities, for example, conventional businesses do not distribute product to people who do not pay for it (the beneficiaries) and expect other people (volunteers) to produce it for free. Unlike a political party, a business is not set up to take over the government of a country, but rather to operate within the legislative framework enacted by a government run by other people. Unlike a religious organisation, a business does not prosper by delivering spiritual and emotional benefits through communal rituals, and is not obliged by its ethic to rely on voluntary donations rather than payments for services. It is possible, in principle, to combine the two roles. One possibility is to run a profit-making organisation whose role is to support the work of a non-profit

DOI: 10.1057/9781137305824

organisation. Some charities, for example, raise funds from the profits of trading organisations such as charity shops. A philanthropist does not need to wait until they have retired from business before giving their money away; for example, they can give their business to their employees by converting their firm into a worker's co-operative. This analysis suggests that conventional business entrepreneurship can be regarded as a special type of leadership in which the leader operates a single organisation devoted mainly to selling material benefits for profit.

Further reading

Two standard business history texts that emphasise the large managerial corporation are

Chandler, A. D. Jr. (1977) *The Visible Hand* (Cambridge, MA: Harvard University Press).

Wilson, J. (1995) *British Business History, 1720–1994* (Manchester: Manchester University Press).

On the contemporary role of small business see

Storey, D. J., and F. J. Greene (2010) *Small Business and Entrepreneurship* (Harlow: Financial Times).

Early work on entrepreneurial history is described in

Cole, A. H. (1974) *The Birth of a New Social Science Discipline: Achievements of the First Generation of American Economic and Business Historians, 1893–1974* (New York: Economic History Association).

On calls for a fresh approach to business history see

Casson, M. and M. Rose (1998) *Institutions and the Evolution of Modern Business* (London: Cass).

Jones, G. G. and W. Friedman (2011) 'Business History: Time for Debate', *Business History Review* 85, 1–8.

For an insightful overview of the modern economic theory of entrepreneurship see

Ricketts, M. (2006) 'Theories of Entrepreneurship: Historical Development and Critical Assessment', in M. Casson, B. Yeung,

A. Basu and N. Wadeson (eds) *Oxford Handbook of Entrepreneurship* (Oxford: Oxford University Press), 33–58.

For a review of entrepreneurial biography and the role of personality see

Corley, T. A. B. (2006) 'Historical Biographies of Entrepreneurs', in M. Casson, B. Yeung, A. Basu and N. Wadeson (eds) *Oxford Handbook of Entrepreneurship* (Oxford: Oxford University Press), 138–60.

Chell, E. (2008) *The Entrepreneurial Personality: A Social Construction* 2nd edn. (London: Routledge).

For early examples of the historical biography of entrepreneurs see

Smiles, S. (1863) *Industrial Biography: Iron Workers and Tool Makers*, (London: John Murray).

Hughes, J. R. T. (1966) *The Vital Few: American Economic Progress and its Protagonists* (Boston: Houghton Mifflin).

DOI: 10.1057/9781137305824

2
Perspectives on Entrepreneurship

Abstract: *Key to understanding entrepreneurship fully is the ability to understand the different ways in which the term is used and the different meanings that it has acquired. Different perspectives on entrepreneurship are examined in this chapter. Popular perceptions of entrepreneurs as business artists, business scientists and business philosophers are examined. The place of the entrepreneur in economic theory is then considered. An entrepreneur is shown to be a person who takes responsibility for difficult decisions and who re-allocates resources to more efficient uses.*

Casson, Mark and Casson, Catherine. *The Entrepreneur in History: From Medieval Merchant to Modern Business Leader.* Basingstoke: Palgrave Macmillan, 2013. DOI: 10.1057/9781137305824.

DOI: 10.1057/9781137305824

2.1   Introduction

Entrepreneurship is a key concept for analysing business and the economy but, like all concepts that achieve popularity, it appears differently to different people. People relate a concept to different contexts and emphasise different aspects of it. Because different people use the same word differently, confusion can result, and sometimes a concept can become discredited as a result. To understand entrepreneurship properly it is important to understand the different ways in which the word is used and the different connotations it has acquired.

This chapter therefore examines entrepreneurship from a number of different perspectives. It begins with perspectives suggested by popular discourse on entrepreneurs, in which they are likened to business artists, business scientists, or business philosophers. It then considers how entrepreneurs appear in the academic business and management literature, as strategists and agents of change. It is suggested that, while all of these perspectives are insightful, they give a distorted picture of the entrepreneur if they are taken too literally.

The place of the entrepreneur in economic theory is then examined. Here too different perspectives can be found, but nevertheless a coherent picture emerges. The entrepreneur appears as an individual who takes responsibility for difficult decisions, such as investment decisions involving product innovation under uncertain conditions. The entrepreneur reallocates resources to more efficient uses, acting on behalf of the owners of the business they control.

2.2   Popular notions of entrepreneurship

2.2.1   The entrepreneur as artist

Artists can be entrepreneurs in the sense that they can make a good livelihood by establishing a studio specialising in a particular kind of work. In the eighteenth century the portrait studio was fashionable, in the nineteenth century the photographic studio and in the twentieth century the craft pottery. Art has long been linked with commerce through the design of labels, packaging, posters and more recently the design of corporate logos and web-sites.

But the fact that artists can become entrepreneurs does not mean that entrepreneurs are artists. The salient point here is that artists are

DOI: 10.1057/9781137305824

regarded as creative individuals and that entrepreneurs can be creative too. Creativity involves coming up with something entirely new. A highly creative person may be described as a genius if they come up with something that nobody else could have done. It is difficult, however, to see inside the head of a genius and work out what is going on. Creativity is perhaps best regarded subjectively. People who come up with something unexpected are said to be creative when other people believe that they would not have come up with something similar themselves. The more surprising, or even shocking, the creative output is, the more creative the individual is deemed to be.

Artists, it is said, see the world differently from other people. This fits with the notion that entrepreneurs can recognise opportunities that other people may miss. Because they view the world through a different lens, the entrepreneur's attention is drawn to phenomena that other people overlook.

Well-known artists are also often said to have a distinctive style. Old master paintings of dubious provenance are often authenticated on the basis of the artist's style, as reflected in the composition, brushwork and use of colour. Indeed, many successful artists have deliberately cultivated a distinctive style that made their work instantly recognisable. Canaletto, Turner and Monet, for example, all achieved great success by developing a style which collectors valued in its own right. An artist's style is similar to a successful brand that may be developed by an entrepreneur.

Many successful entrepreneurs have become prominent art collectors, and bequeathed their collections to public galleries (e.g. Henry Tate) or created galleries of their own (e.g. William Hesketh Lever). Art has been used as an inspiration for advertising campaigns; a recent example being the Saatchi brothers' modern art collection in London.

2.2.2   The entrepreneur as scientist

Steve Jobs of Apple and Bill Gates of Microsoft both personify the link between science and entrepreneurship. Earlier examples include James Watt, who designed and produced an improved stationary steam engine and William Armstrong, who pioneered hydraulic power. The link between science and entrepreneurship is complex, however. Inventive scientists have often collaborated with entrepreneurs rather than become entrepreneurs themselves. The national patent systems established in the nineteenth century were designed specifically to allow scientists to sell the right to their inventions to independent entrepreneurs, leaving the scientist free to concentrate on doing their research. During the Industrial Revolution in Britain many key innovations were effected through business partnerships between entrepreneurs like Richard Arkwright and artisan inventors exploiting their mechanical skills.

Today the use of science to develop new technologies for commercialisation is well understood. Politicians everywhere emphasise the need for a strong science base to promote competitiveness in high-technology industries. However, the application of entrepreneurship to science is one thing, and the application of science to entrepreneurship is another. Should entrepreneurs not only collaborate with scientists, but become scientific themselves in their approach to business decisions? What does it mean for an entrepreneur to be scientific in this way, and is it even desirable?

There is a good historical precedent for suggesting that entrepreneurs should not attempt to be scientific in their approach to business. Immediately before World War II there was considerable interest in making business scientific. Statisticians were employed to forecast sales and to plan inventories, and accountants were employed to estimate rates of return on new investments. Psychologists analysed the motivations of employees and time and motion studies were carried out on production lines. Advertising campaigns were no longer based just on striking images and extravagant claims but, allegedly, on a deep understanding of consumer psychology. Managers in large firms came to see themselves as a professional elite; they developed procedures for making decisions involving time-consuming research and lengthy committee meetings. A mistaken notion evolved that by using scientific methods managers could not only forecast the future but also control it.

These tendencies were reinforced by World War II, and by the postwar fashion for national economic planning based on target levels of output. Keynesian economic management, it was believed, would assure full employment and a steady rate of economic growth in the national economy, removing residual uncertainty from the business environment. Managers of large firms therefore became planners, working within a planned economy that provided them with an environment of certainty. There was certainty, however, only so long as other firms fulfilled their plans. Once they failed to do so, the plans basically collapsed. Crisis ensued, and improvisation became the order of the day. Entrepreneurs emerged to rescue the situation. As large firms foundered in the 1970s,

DOI: 10.1057/9781137305824

small firms emerged to replace them. Their success, it seemed was based on instinct and intuition rather than scientific thinking. Their business decisions were reasonable, rather than rational in some scientific sense. The moral of this story has become embedded in popular culture, and still remains influential today.

The real moral of the story, however, is more prosaic. It is that uncertainty can never be entirely eliminated from the business environment and that an organisation composed of people cannot be managed as though it were a collection of machines. The moral is not that irrational decisions are better than rational decisions, but rather that truly rational decisions are ones that take account of uncertainty and of human fallibility.

There is, therefore, a case to be made that entrepreneurs should be scientific in their approach to business. For this purpose, science needs to be defined, not in terms of the subjects it encompasses – such as physics and chemistry – but as a method of study. A scientist strives for objective detachment towards the phenomena they study. Whenever possible they set out to measure phenomena under carefully controlled conditions that can be replicated by others. For this purpose they design experiments which are conducted in a laboratory. Experiments are often designed to test a hypothesis. A hypothesis is a proposition, normally derived from, or suggested by, some theory, that predicts what will be observed under certain conditions. An experiment can refute a hypothesis by generating evidence that conflicts with these predictions. It cannot confirm a hypothesis with absolute certainty, however, since it is impossible to be sure that future experiments will not reveal anomalies that earlier experiments missed.

It could be argued that entrepreneurs cannot be scientists because science studies natural objects and entrepreneurs have to deal with people. People still reveal patterns in their behaviour, however – e.g. they purchase larger quantities when prices fall – and such patterns are, in principle, no different to patterns observed in nature. It could also be argued that entrepreneurs cannot carry out experiments under controlled conditions. Not all scientists can do so either, however; cosmologists and evolutionary biologists, for example, cannot easily collect data from laboratory experiments, but have to deal directly with the world in all its complexity. Entrepreneurs can, in fact, perform experiments, as when they test market products on representative panels of consumers. Indeed, it can be argued that entrepreneurs test a hypothesis every time they launch a new product. A typical hypothesis is that the new product

DOI: 10.1057/9781137305824

is an improvement on the old one, and that consumers will therefore be willing to pay a premium for it. In this experiment 'the market decides'. Consumers evaluate the product, and their decisions are final: if they approve then output will be expanded, and if they do not then production will be shut down. The entrepreneur does not necessarily believe that the hypothesis is true, but they believe that the probability that it is true is sufficiently high to make the experiment worthwhile.

An entrepreneur who sets out to act as a scientist will think very carefully about their hypothesis. Is the hypothesis that the product is better, or that it is cheaper to produce, or is it a combination of the two? Is the hypothesis that everyone will want to buy the product, or only certain types of people? Prior to product launch, the entrepreneur will attempt to test their hypothesis through market research and small-scale production. Potential customers may be surveyed by questionnaire, and then a small number of samples produced. This will provide an indication of production costs and also allow the trial product to be offered to consumers for their use. Once the product is launched the scientific entrepreneur will capture as much information as possible about who has purchased the product (e.g. by offering special guarantees) and whether they have encountered any problems with it (by offering a subsidised after-sales service). This feedback of information means that even if the product fails, a new and even better version can be quickly produced.

2.2.3   The entrepreneur as philosopher

The image of the entrepreneur as a person of action immersed in their business activities suggests that they could be regarded as the very antithesis of a philosopher. The popular image of the philosopher is that of someone who has retired from the world, and speculates about it rather than participates in it. Despite this, however, there are grounds for arguing that a successful entrepreneur needs their business judgement to be underpinned by a sound philosophy.

Philosophy has always been a potent intellectual force. Most influential politicians have built their careers by popularising an ideology that has philosophical roots. The great political contest between capitalism and socialism that characterised much of the late nineteenth and early twentieth century had its roots in philosophical debates over the place of private property in an industrialising economy. Much of the recent literature on entrepreneurship has a distinctive philosophical perspective,

DOI: 10.1057/9781137305824

and continues this great debate is a slightly different form. Some writers take the view that entrepreneurship can only thrive under free market capitalism, whilst others believe that the state needs to intervene in industry to promote technological innovation.

Philosophy encourages critical thinking, requiring people to re-examine widely accepted propositions to see if they are sound. From a deductive point of view, do the conclusions follow from the assumptions? From an inductive point of view, does the evidence support the hypothesis? Are there alternative assumptions that are equally plausible that might lead to different conclusions? Is there more than one way of interpreting the evidence? Does the evidence directly confirm the hypothesis, or could it interpreted differently, and used to support some other hypothesis instead?

Successful entrepreneurs often question conventional wisdom. The willingness to challenge conventional wisdom underpins their creativity. It is impossible to think creatively if your aim is simply to conform with prevailing opinion and to emulate other people's behaviour. By grounding their opinions on general philosophical considerations, an entrepreneur may well come to a different conclusion from other people. Being an entrepreneur as well as a philosopher, they may well put their dissident opinion into practice by acting in a manner that seems unwise, or downright foolish to other people.

Not all entrepreneurs who are advocates of some philosophy are necessarily philosophical in this sense, however. Some political philosophies are popular with entrepreneurs for purely self-serving reasons. The statement that 'entrepreneurs are wealth-creators', for example, is often proclaimed as a philosophical insight, but unfortunately ignores the fact that anyone who works is potentially a wealth creator, including people who do not work for money. Successful entrepreneurs do not necessarily 'talk' philosophy, but they act philosophically by challenging conventional wisdom on the fundamental grounds that it is not necessarily true.

This helps to explain why entrepreneurs are sometimes unpopular and seen as socially disruptive. They simply cannot bring themselves to agree with a consensus view that they regard as unsound.

2.2.4   The entrepreneur as an agent of change

The concept of the entrepreneur as an agent of change is popular in contemporary management literature. It embodies a very important truth,

DOI: 10.1057/9781137305824

which is simply that it is often possible to improve upon the status quo, and that not everyone accepts this.

It is a widely held belief that things have to be the way they are, and could not be otherwise. The fact that they are the way they are appears to confirm the view that they have to be that way. People are usually unhappy with counter-factual exercises in which things are imagined to be different from the way that they actually are. Successful entrepreneurs, on the other hand, appear to have no difficulty with counter-factual exercises. They instinctively challenge the view that things cannot be different. Like a good philosopher, they are willing to consider all the logical possibilities of a situation, and not just the outcome that happens to materialise at the time.

The fact that things could be different, however, does not mean that they necessarily become better – they might become worse. Change and progress are two different things. Even where improvement is possible, it may not be achieved. Attempts at improvement can result in spectacular failures which leave a situation worse than before. Firms operating in stagnating markets have gone bankrupt through failed diversification into high-growth areas, while information technology initiatives in government departments have left services to the public in disarray. Despite all the hype to the contrary, no-change policies such as sticking to traditional markets still have much to recommend them.

Change is particularly difficult to effect in large organisations. Such organisations typically employ a complex internal division of labour in which different types of specialist liaise with each other. A single change may therefore involve the re-definition of a large number of roles. An entrepreneur who considers himself as an agent of change may not fully understand the nuances of all the different roles. As a result, they may mistake the legitimate concerns of the staff for self-serving opposition to change. This can impair consultation, which in turn results in loss of key staff and disappointing outcomes.

When large business organisations first emerged towards the end of the nineteenth century, the chief executives who ran them had usually risen through the ranks, and therefore had 'bottom-up' experience of the organisation. Furthermore, specialist knowledge within the organisation was acquired mainly through experience rather than through higher education. As a result, the problems of managing specialist employees were less acute than today, when chief executives with lower educational qualifications than their specialist employees are parachuted from other organisations with a remit for change.

'Change agents' often see their role as one of overcoming a succession of obstacles placed in their path. Overcoming the obstacles becomes a test of will-power, in which aggression is increasingly directed by the 'change agent' against members of the organisation who are seen to be opposing change. Even when successful, change usually comes slowly. Steady change allows each step to be consolidated before the next is begun. 'Change agents' who become impatient may attempt to change things too quickly. Ironically, change designed to adapt the organisation to external threats may become an internal threat to the organisation.

'Change agent' entrepreneurs may in turn be pressurised by external stakeholders to push through rapid change, thereby creating 'change for the sake of change'. An entrepreneur who has no changes to push through may themselves be changed for someone who has. Change is no longer a response to a problem, but has become the problem itself. Ironically, the true entrepreneur becomes someone who can recognise the true problem and can take control in order to stop, or even reverse the change. Recent moves to 'make banks boring again' could be regarded as a case in point.

2.2.5　The entrepreneur as strategist

The strategist, like the 'change agent', is another prominent figure in modern culture. Like the 'change agent', they behave pro-actively and stay 'ahead of the game'. The modern resurgence of interest in strategy began with the decline of Western industrial firms in the 1970s, as mentioned earlier. Strategy was developed as a business discipline in order to alert complacent bureaucratic managers in large firms to the continual threat from new sources of competition; in the case of Europe and the US, this referred to Japan.

In military terms, therefore, business strategy emphasised a defensive posture. It recommended managers to identify key rivals, monitor them closely, and remain alert to changes in the business environment. Strategy was presented as a cerebral activity. Intelligent strategy was founded on a deep understanding of the fundamental drivers of competition. While competition was a general process, it took specific forms in specific industries, which managers in these industries needed to appreciate.

DOI: 10.1057/9781137305824

During the 1990s, however, the popularisation of strategy by consulting firms had led to a trivialisation of strategic thinking. The emphasis switched to aggressive strategies of globalisation. Conquering the world market became the new strategic imperative, which was linked to increasingly absurd objectives such as a firm establishing a subsidiary in every foreign country.

Strategy also became disconnected from drivers of industry competition. It became an aspect of entrepreneurial vision instead. When shared with employees this vision became a powerful force and, just in case the employees did not get the message, it could be displayed on posters, office stationery and coffee mugs. Charismatic leadership, based on a vision charged with emotion that was openly shared with employees, became a superficial indicator of success. With sufficient charisma, it was claimed, the entrepreneur could over-ride the economic forces driving industry competition, and achieve whatever they aspired to.

A popular vision centred on a firm becoming 'number one' in their industry. In practice many firms were clearly 'number twos' (at best), but for them there was another strategy – joint ventures. Ostensibly joint ventures were a strategy for exploiting synergies, whereby two number twos added together made a number one. In practice, however, many joint ventures were short-lived and, where they succeeded, one of the two firms often emerged as the clear winner. Charismatic entrepreneurs did not fare much better; many lasted only a short time in their roles. The basic drivers of industry competition re-asserted their authority, and the entrepreneurs had to settle for a golden handshake and a pension.

2.3 Theories of entrepreneurship

2.3.1 Introduction

Having considered some of the more popular ideas about entrepreneurship, it is time to focus on a more rigorous approach. The agenda is to develop a concept of the entrepreneur which can inform historical appreciation of the importance of the role. As far as possible, the concept should be institution-free, so that it can be applied not only across different centuries but across different countries and cultures too. It is no good, for example, defining an entrepreneur as the owner or manager of a small firm, as many people do today, because the firm as we know

DOI: 10.1057/9781137305824

it now did not really exist until the middle of the nineteenth century. Before that time, joint-stock ownership by large numbers of shareholders enjoying limited liability for losses did not exist except for a few specially chartered firms.

The easiest way to develop an institution-free account of entrepreneurship is to focus on the economic function of the entrepreneur. An entrepreneur is what an entrepreneur does, in other words. This approach has proved very useful in other contexts, for example, the definition of money. Credit cards were used almost exclusively by business travellers until the 1970s, and bank notes were little used, except for large transactions, before the 1820s. Defining money in terms of bank deposits and credit card balances is therefore of little use historically but, on the other hand, defining money purely in terms of coin or bullion is inadequate for modern times. Defining money as a specialised medium of exchange and store of value covers everything, however.

Various functions have been ascribed to the entrepreneur in the theoretical literature, including innovation, risk-bearing and opportunity-seeking, and these are discussed below. It is useful to begin with the most abstract of the functions associated with the entrepreneur, however – namely coordination.

2.3.2   The entrepreneur as coordinator

Coordination contrasts sharply with the ideas discussed above because the focus is not on the entrepreneur's own ideas and thinking, but on behaviour of the economy. The basic point is that it does not matter what great ideas an entrepreneur has if they have no impact on the economy. To have an impact on the economy they must change the way that resources are used. The intervention of the entrepreneur must switch resources from one use to another. Furthermore, people should be better off as a result. If they are worse then it would be better that the change had never been made and that the entrepreneur had never acted.

But how can we say that people as a whole are better off? If one person is better off but another person is worse off, how do we weigh the two effects against each other? In the absence of an objective measure of welfare, interpersonal comparisons are difficult to make. It is reasonable to suggest, however, that if one person is made better off and no-one else is made worse off then society as a whole is better off; this is known as Pareto improvement, and is the concept of coordination used below.

DOI: 10.1057/9781137305824

If people are rational and reasonably well-informed, then if they accept some take-it or leave-it proposition it may be inferred that they preferred the proposition to the status quo and are therefore better off by accepting it. If, therefore, an entrepreneur puts two different take-it or leave-it propositions to two different people and both accept then it may be assumed that both are better off. If, in addition, the entrepreneur themselves derive a profit (pecuniary or otherwise) from their intervention then it may be assumed that they are better off as well. This implies that if a person buys a product from someone at a low price and sells that product to someone else at a high price then everyone is better off. For example, if an entrepreneur notices a sought-after work of art in a local antique shop, buys it, and sells it to a specialist dealer in a nearby city then the art-work finishes up in the hand of someone who values it more than did its original owner. The antique dealer was happy to sell, the city leader was happy to buy, and the entrepreneur was happy to make a profit.

This may seem a perverse result, because if the two people (the dealers) had traded directly without the intermediation of the entrepreneur then they would have been even better off because they could have shared the profit between them. They may not have been in direct contact with each other, however. It may be only because the entrepreneur knew both of them separately that the opportunity for arbitrage was recognised. The entrepreneur could still have refused to take a profit, however. But if the entrepreneur only got to know the parties because of the profit potential, the trade would never have taken place. In any case, the entrepreneur may have incurred costs in making contact, or in transporting the product, and so a portion of the profit may have been absorbed by expenses. If there had been no margin then the trade could not have taken place

This example may seem naïve, but the basic principle is sound, and more realistic examples involving many people are easily constructed.

2.3.3 The entrepreneur as opportunity-seeker

Considerable debate has arisen over where profit opportunities come from. The example above makes the answer clear. Opportunities arise because information in the economy is distributed across different people. The local shopkeeper knows local people who would pay a modest price, but not the city dealer who would pay a higher price. The city dealer does not know the local shopkeeper. The entrepreneur knows

DOI: 10.1057/9781137305824

both the shopkeeper and the city dealer, and this makes it possible for them to organise a trade. The distribution of information explains why the city dealer did not buy the picture directly from the shopkeeper – he did not know where to find it.

In economic terms, the initial situation is a disequilibrium because there is an unexploited opportunity. Sooner or later this opportunity will be recognised, and then the situation will change. The prospect of profit provides a stimulus to change. Because the situation creates an incentive for change, it is not an equilibrium. On the other hand, the final situation is an equilibrium, because there is no longer an incentive for change.

An opportunity can arise at any time. Antique dealers prosper when people move house or die, and their valuables are cleared out. Natural volatility in the environment driven by numerous mundane events generates a steady stream of unpredictable opportunities. The economy is therefore is continuous disequilibrium. At any time there is a stock of unexploited opportunities, and a flow of profit generated by the opportunities that are being exploited. In the long run the economy will adjust towards a state in which the number of new opportunities created is equal, on average, to the number of opportunities exploited for profit. Thus the number of unexploited opportunities is stable even though the stock of opportunities is constantly turning over.

Secrecy is crucial to the appropriation of profit by the entrepreneur. If the entrepreneur told the local shopkeeper that they intended to sell the picture to the city dealer then the shopkeeper might withdraw the picture from sale so that the shopkeeper could sell it to the dealer themselves. The entrepreneur's indiscretion will eliminate their profit.

If two entrepreneurs discover the same opportunity at the same time then the outcome will be similar. Competition between them will bid up the price to the local shopkeeper until one of the entrepreneurs is forced to withdraw. This may leave the other entrepreneur with just sufficient margin to reimburse the cost of selling on the picture to the dealer, but neither entrepreneur will make a profit. In prospecting for opportunities, therefore, first mover advantage is normally required in order to appropriate profit.

This result suggests a paradox: that it is monopoly and not competition that stimulates entrepreneurship. The paradox is resolved by distinguishing between competition in discovering opportunities and competition in exploiting them. Competition in discovery combined with monopoly in exploitation generates the best outcome for the economy as a whole.

DOI: 10.1057/9781137305824

In a volatile economy opportunities will be generated at a faster rate than a single entrepreneur could cope with. Furthermore, opportunities are so diverse that it normally requires a range of entrepreneurs with different skills to exploit them. Competition builds a field of entrepreneurs that is matched to the rate at which opportunities become available. Economic theory suggests that the number of entrepreneurs will expand until the marginal entrepreneur (the last to enter) earns just enough to compensate them for the effort involved. If entrepreneurship is a fulltime occupation, then an entrepreneur must be compensated for the loss of earnings in their best alternative occupation. If entrepreneurship is more enjoyable than the alternative, however, then the entrepreneur may be willing to accept a lower reward. On the other hand, if entrepreneurship is perceived as very risky (e.g. earnings are volatile) then a higher reward may be required instead.

Suppose that the main alternative to entrepreneurship is routine work. If an entrepreneur is very good at discovering opportunities and not very good at routine jobs then they will earn far more as an entrepreneur than they would in an alternative occupation. In economic terminology, they earn a competitive rent that is equal to the difference between their earnings as an entrepreneur and their earnings in routine work. Such people will be the first to enter the entrepreneurship field. By contrast the marginal entrepreneur is equally good at entrepreneurship and routine work; they receive no economic rent as an entrepreneur. Because their occupational choice is finely balanced, they will leave the field if the prospects for discovering opportunities diminish.

Using this approach, it is easy to explain why the supply of entrepreneurs has increased substantially since the 1970s. Before the 1970s the economic environment was perceived as very stable. Risks were low and it was easy for managers to plan for the future. Most of the big opportunities had already been exploited by established firms. When emerging global competition undermined the performance of established firms, opportunities were created for smaller firms to step in. An industry composed of a large number of small firms would be far more flexible than an industry dominated by a small number of large firms. Greater volatility stimulated a flow of opportunities that small firms were able to exploit.

2.3.4 The entrepreneur as innovator

In the previous example the product handled by the entrepreneur already existed. The entrepreneur simply changed its use. In the case of

DOI: 10.1057/9781137305824

the painting the change of use was effected simply by a change of ownership brokered by the entrepreneur.

The entrepreneur becomes a more potent force when they innovate the product that is traded. The entrepreneur imagines a product that does not yet exist and brings it into being. But why invent a new product? The answer is presumably that there is something wrong with existing products. An economist would say that there is some need or desire that existing products do not adequately fulfil. People need food but do not like what is on the existing menu; or they desire to be entertained, but don't find existing performers very amusing. There is a problem, in other words: a gap between the aspirations of individuals and the reality of what is currently available. In this context the entrepreneur appears as a problem-solver, and their solution is a product innovation.

But why cannot people solve their problems for themselves? Why must someone else do it for them? The answer is that it is usually more efficient that way. Many people are too busy to invent new products; other may simply lack the imagination or the technical skill. It therefore pays people who are good at innovation to specialise in it, and this creates a role for the innovative entrepreneur.

Suppose that the entrepreneur has a friend who has a problem: writing a book makes their back stiff. The author cannot think of a solution but the entrepreneur can visualise one: a special ergonomic back rest. The entrepreneur needs a physiotherapist to design it and a skilled craftsman to make it. The entrepreneur pays the physiotherapist a fee in return for exclusive rights to exploit the design. They pay the craftsman for a day's work and sell the back rest to their friend.

So far this is just conventional coordination, but involving multiple parties: the customer, the designer, the craftsman and the entrepreneur. As before, the entrepreneur is the nexus because everyone makes contracts with the entrepreneur.

But the entrepreneur can do much better than this. At the moment there is just one customer, as before. But the entrepreneur may recognise that there are many customers: a high proportion of all authors are likely to have back problems. The problem is generic in other words. If the entrepreneur's design can be standardised then their solution will be generic too. The profit opportunity can be scaled up. Indeed it will work even better at a large scale because of production economies: they can employ a team of craftsman full time instead of relying on a single craftsman performing a one-off job.

DOI: 10.1057/9781137305824

The problem facing the entrepreneur is now different. Initially they were in contact with their customer, and had to find a solution to that customer's problem. Now they have solved the problem but they have to make contact with other customers. They have to identify all the authors with back problems. This is a marketing problem. There is no established market for back support for authors, and so the entrepreneur has to develop one. To make contact with customers the entrepreneur may advertise in an art magazine, or attend an art show with a demonstration product. The entrpreneur must advertise a price which is basically the same for everyone, unless they can prove they are in some category that qualifies for a discount. If the price is high then the profit margin will be high but few people will be willing to buy, while if it is low than the margin will be low but the quantity will be higher. The entrepreneur must trade-off price against quantity without being sure exactly what the trade-off is like.

This example shows that innovation involves two problems rather than one. One is to develop the design and technology to solve the customer's problem and embody the solution in a product that can be sold. The other is to make contact with a large group of customers and persuade them to purchase the product. Innovation and marketing are inextricably linked.

The innovative entrepreneur now coordinates the actions of many different people: the designer, a team of craftsmen and a large group of customers. They may not even know the customers' identities if the customers simply call into a shop and take the product away. Just as before, the parties involved could, in principle, trade directly with each other, but the entrepreneur prevents this by keeping the customers and craftsmen apart. The contribution of the entrepreneur is to recognise the generic nature of the problem. They extract a reward for this by setting a margin between the cost of production and the selling price.

Innovation therefore introduces two additional elements into coordination: problem-solving and market-making. The entrepreneur identifies a generic problem – i.e. a problem that potentially affects an entire class of people. The easier it is to identify the class of people affected and to make contact with them, the easier it is to target market-making activity. Market-making activity involves establishing a supply chain and devising a pricing strategy. Supply chain issues can be quite complex, involving decisions on whether to produce in-house or subcontract, whether to sell by shop or mail order, and what standard of after-sales service to

DOI: 10.1057/9781137305824

provide. Solving the customers' problem is only the start: implementing the solution is necessary to finish the job.

2.3.5   The entrepreneur as pre-emptor

Innovation introduces a risk of imitation. If an entrepreneur identifies a one-off opportunity to buy a product cheap and re-sell it dear, as in the case of the painting, then once the deal has been made the opportunity is exhausted. Moving quickly pre-empts any rival. But this is not the case with innovation. Innovation introduces a stream of opportunities to sell a new product to many different people. Product development may incur substantial set-up costs that can be recovered only from a large volume of sales. It may take several years for the innovator to break even. Yet as soon as customers take delivery, some may realise that they could profit by producing and selling a similar product themselves. They can take apart the product they have purchased and 'reverse-engineer' an imitation. They may even discover improvements that could render the original obsolete. This is not the only threat: once the innovator has begun to earn large profits, they will attract attention from other entrepreneurs, who may decide to enter the market too. Entrants may 'head hunt' key employees of the innovator to acquire their inside knowledge, thereby weakening the innovator at the same time that they strengthen their own capabilities. How can the entrepreneur pre-empt the opportunity when there is plenty of time for others to invade their market before they have made a profit?

Many innovators use patents to protect themselves against imitation, but the scope of the patent system is limited; it works much better in some industries, such as engineering, than in others, such as fashion and design. It is often possible to invent around a patent; e.g. once a new drug has demonstrated that a medical condition can be cured, rival drugs using similar principles but different chemicals may appear on the market. Registered trademarks and copyright also provide only limited protection. Trademarks protect the brand rather than the product, and evidence suggests that customers cannot always tell the difference between an authentic product and a cheap imitation with a similar sounding name. Confidentiality agreements can be used to deter key employees from joining employers in the same industry.

Innovators therefore need a comprehensive range of strategies to deter imitation. Some innovators rush out large volumes of new product to

DOI: 10.1057/9781137305824

saturate the market before potential rivals have a chance to catch up. This is appropriate for long-life (durable) products where repeat purchasing is low, but it is also risky because if the product is unsuccessful then the innovator will be left with large amounts of unsold stock. With short-life (perishable) products, where repeat purchasing is common, existing customers can be locked in using loyalty schemes based on a strong brand image, and special discounts on subsequent purchases. Innovators sometimes integrate forward into distribution in order to prevent rivals gaining access to their customers, e.g. major film studios have sometimes bought up local cinema chains to prevent rivals from showing competing films. Forward integration can also be useful in policing trademark infringement.

Rivals also can be locked out by the pre-emption of key resource inputs. In the nineteenth century many European industrial entrepreneurs 'locked out' foreign rivals by monopolising the supplies of the raw materials used in their industry. In the inter-war period entrepreneurs in Europe and the US lobbied for protection of the home market as a device for excluding foreign competition from manufacturing industries; they argued that profits from a protected domestic market were essential to fund the research and development required for innovation.

The most creative way for an innovator to protect their position is to regularly improve their product and thereby keep one step ahead of the competition. This is particularly true where radical innovations are concerned. The full potential of a radical innovation is rarely captured at the outset. Experience gained with the first version of the product can be used to design a second version, and so on. Products move through a life cycle, in which the first version is sold as a low-volume luxury item, the second as a moderate-volume aspirational purchase, and the third as a high-volume mass-produced value-for-money item that is promoted as a social necessity.

Many innovators fail to follow their products through the life cycle, however. Innovators who found an industry are often pre-occupied with low-volume sales. Their radicalism is focused on technology rather than a vision of the market. Radical technological innovations are usually greeted with a degree of scepticism, and as a result the market is initially very small. Innovations like main-frame computers, steam traction engines and motor cars were initially produced in very small quantities, and were sold to wealthy individuals and institutions at very high prices. Experiences with the initial products validated the technology and

DOI: 10.1057/9781137305824

suggested ways that it could be improved. But sometimes the pioneering entrepreneur could not visualise additional uses of the product. People working in other fields began to realise that the product could address a broader range of problems, and it was they who spotted the opportunity to widen the market.

Widening the market for a pioneering product requires it to be made affordable; it needs to be produced cheaply, and to facilitate distribution and utilisation, it often needs to be made more compact too. Many products that began as bulky, expensive craft-built products of a highly specialised nature finish up, after several re-designs, as compact cheap mass-produced products that are very versatile. Versatility allows the product to meets the needs of many different types of users, and is often achieved by configuring the product as a multicomponent good; the modern mobile phone is a notable example of this.

The way that the life cycle of the product is managed affects the expected profitability of innovation. To maximise life-time profit, an innovator must form at an early stage an assessment of ultimate size of the market, and this requires them to have a proper appreciation of all the uses to which the product can be put. The innovator must not under-estimate the incentive for imitation, but must act in such a way that imitators are deterred. Continuous improvement is therefore required. Improvement must proceed along a number of dimensions. Improvement should not be too focused on technological wizardry, which may over-complicate the product and increase its price. It needs to impress everyday users who may have little understanding of the technology on which the product is based, and not just appeal to specialists. Simplification is usually more appropriate; this can often be achieved through modularisation, in which complications are confined to individual modules rather than the product as a whole.

If the innovator fails to assess the market properly, however, then imitators will appear. In order to circumvent patents they may not imitate directly, but find some other technological solution to the same problem. Once a cheaper and more versatile product has been launched, demand for the original version will disappear. The imitator may in turn be displaced by another imitator with an even more radical view of the market. Since the imitators are taking a different view of the market, and are improving the technology, they may be regarded as entrepreneurs in their own right.

DOI: 10.1057/9781137305824

With imitation, profit from the original innovation will be spread more thinly, with the entrepreneurs at the later stages of the product cycle potentially making the greatest profit. The overall profit extracted by the entrepreneurs will tend to be lower too, because competition between them will drive down price and thereby pass on a large share of the benefits of the innovation to the customers instead.

Effective deterrence of imitation will therefore encourage entrepreneurs to make radical innovations, and those entrepreneurs that succeed can make enormous profits. There will be plenty of radical innovations, but their adoption and diffusion may be impeded by monopoly pricing, and this may have adverse effects on the rest of the economy. Easy imitation, on the other hand, will discourage radical innovation, and encourage entrepreneurs to focus on 'me-too' versions of other people's products instead. Pricing will be competitive and profits low. Government industrial policy – in particular policies relating to intellectual property rights – are important with regard to imitation. The trade-off between encouraging innovation and promoting competition has, not surprisingly, proved problematic for many governments, and after centuries of debate there is still no consensus on the subject.

2.3.6   The entrepreneur as judgemental decision-maker

Innovation involves substantial set-up costs. Yet customer response to a novel product is always difficult to predict. Customers may not know whether they want a product until they have tried it. Both development costs and production costs must therefore be incurred before sales revenue can be generated. These costs are sunk: they cannot be recovered if customers reject the product.

The economic literature on innovation recognises that entrepreneurs can make mistakes, but it tends to assume that the mistake is always not to innovate – to miss an opportunity, in other words. Little attention is given to mistaken innovation. Yet the history of innovation is littered with mistakes. Post-war British aviation is a case in point. Britain pioneered the passenger jet aircraft, the vertical take-off fighter plane and developed a range of guided missiles, but by the 1970s most of these projects had failed.

There are two mistakes to be made in innovation: to miss an opportunity, and to attempt to exploit an opportunity that does not actually exist. These two mistakes apply, indeed, to any decision. In the theory of statistics, wasting resources on an imaginary opportunity is an example of a Type I error, in which the null hypothesis 'There is no opportunity' is wrongly rejected, whilst missing an opportunity is a Type II error in which the null hypothesis is wrongly accepted.

One error may be more expensive that the other. Suppose that an innovation costs £1million, and generates £5million in revenue if successful and nothing if it fails. If it fails the costs cannot be recovered. The cost of a Type I error is therefore £1million, wasted on the costs of an unsuccessful innovation, while the cost of a Type II error is £4million, the profit that could have be earned if a successful innovation had been made. In this case the cost of a Type II error is four times the cost of a Type I error. Thus if the entrepreneur believes that the odds in favour of a successful innovation are 50:50 then expected profit is maximised by making the innovation despite the risk involved. The expected profit of innovation is £1.5million and the expected profit of not innovating is zero. If, on the other hand, the costs rose to £3million, then the cost of a Type I error would rise accordingly, and the cost of a Type II error fall to £2million, and it would no longer pay to invest. The expected loss from innovation would be £0.5million, while the loss from innovating would again be zero.

With perfect information it is possible to eliminate both types of error. But where information is incomplete, there is always a risk of error. Different sources of information may lead to different errors. Consider the different sources of information available on innovation opportunities in a particular industry. One source is a major customer of the industry. The customer is dissatisfied with the current range of products on offer and knows what sort of products they would prefer, but they have no idea how they might be produced, and cannot understand why such products are not already available. This source can recognise immediately any innovation that will have a ready market, but cannot advise on implementation. Another source is a technical expert on the industry. This source can identify with certainty any technology that is liable to fail. But they have no information about the state of the market.

When costs are low and potential profits high, it pays to consult the first source, since their ability to identify demand controls the most serious error of missing a genuine opportunity. On the other hand, when costs are higher and profits are lower it is better to consult the second source, since their ability to identify inappropriate technologies controls the most serious error of exploiting an imaginary opportunity.

DOI: 10.1057/9781137305824

Both these strategies will normally out-perform uninformed strategies such as 'Always invest whatever the circumstances', 'Never invest', or 'Toss a coin to decide'. The best strategy, however, will tend to be one that combines both sources of information. An entrepreneur who consults both sources and synthesises the information from them can control both types of error. They are likely to out-perform everyone else.

In general there are many sources of information relevant to any potential innovation, and there are many potential entrepreneurs, all of whom have access to some particular subset of this information. This means that different entrepreneurs would take the same decision differently. This does not mean that they are irrational, for each of them may act perfectly rationally conditional on the information they possess. In some cases entrepreneurs may have similar information but may interpret it in different ways. Two entrepreneurs might observe that customers are shunning some new product introduced by a rival; one may believe that the market is saturated and infer that there is no demand for the product, while the other may infer that customers are interested in the product but do not like the packaging. Each responds in a different way and the market outcome determines who was correct. Thus different basic assumptions, combined with different information, cause entrepreneurs in similar situations to take different decisions.

This may be summed up by saying that entrepreneurial decision-making is a judgemental activity. To an outside observer the behaviour of an entrepreneur may seem unusual, and even inexplicable, but that is because they do not know on what information the entrepreneur is acting. The entrepreneur may know more than the observer, but it is possible that they may know less. They may be acting on assumptions with which the observer would disagree, but the observer might have to admit that they cannot prove the assumptions to be wrong, and that they might well turn out to be right even though the observer does not think that they will.

Judgement is involved, not only in taking decisions, but in deciding to become an entrepreneur and, having decided to become an entrepreneur it is involved in deciding in which field of the economy to operate. The economy as a whole will perform best when each innovation decision is taken by the person best equipped to take it, but nobody really knows who that person is. Different people have different opinions on the subject because it is a judgemental decision.

DOI: 10.1057/9781137305824

In a free society coordinated by market forces anyone can decide to become an entrepreneur. On a very small scale, they could buy some second-hand goods from house clearance and set up at a car boot sale or market stall. This will give them a chance to discover whether they really have the entrepreneurial abilities that they believe they possess. Ambitious entrepreneurs may raise capital from family or friends to expand their business, or offer their services as chief executive of an established firm. Whether they get a loan from their friends, or the job they want, will depend on their reputation, i.e. on whether other people rate their abilities as highly as they rate them themselves.

Entrepreneurs do not merely take judgemental decisions, but actively specialise in taking judgemental decisions. Everyone takes judgemental decisions at some stage of their life, whether it is choosing a partner, or moving house to take a new job. But entrepreneurs specialise in taking such decisions by inviting other people to place their resources under their control. A person who invests in an entrepreneur's business places their resources under the entrepreneur's control as, to a more limited extent, does an employee who places their own labour at the disposal of the entrepreneur in return for a wage. People are reluctant to place their resources under someone's control unless they trust them on the basis of their reputation.

Luck as well as judgement undoubtedly plays a role in entrepreneurial success and failure, but in the long run those who lack judgement will fail too often and decide to take the safer option of paid employment instead, while those with good judgement will prosper. Some may sell out and retire in luxury, whilst misers and workaholics may continue working because they can think of nothing they would rather do. Many may remain content to run small businesses as lifestyle options, or as a means of providing employment for their children.

Different entrepreneurs will tend to be good at taking different types of decision. In the long run survivors will tend to specialise in the sorts of roles in which they perform best, according to industry and size of organisation. The expertise they accumulate will improve their decision-making ability, but possibly blinker them to relevant changes in related areas of the economy.

Economic efficiency requires that entrepreneurs are matched to the most appropriate decisions according to their ability. There is no single institution that is dedicated to this matching process. The market for business professionals, however, together with the financial markets,

DOI: 10.1057/9781137305824

have a crucial role in allocating resources between entrepreneurs and holding them to account for the way in which they use them. Both these markets, in turn, rely heavily on reputation in matching individual entrepreneurs to specific decision-making roles.

2.3.7 The entrepreneur as risk-taker

The relationship between entrepreneurship and risk-taking has been extensively discussed in the theoretical literature. Innovation is a risky process, as noted above, because it is easy for mistakes to be made. It therefore seems obvious that the entrepreneur is a risk-taker. Despite this, it can be argued that only a small proportion of this risk is borne by the entrepreneur.

Risk is endemic in entrepreneurship. The entrepreneur who buys and re-sells a painting cannot normally synchronise the purchase and sale. There is a period during which he owns a painting but lacks a customer for it. It is also possible that the painting could be damaged in transit to the purchaser. This risk is insurable, however, so the entrepreneur does not have to bear it. It is generally agreed that entrepreneurs only bear uninsurable risks.

It is possible that the other risk could be insured as well, however. Suppose that the entrepreneur establishes a firm in which other people invest and then buys the picture through his firm; then if the picture cannot be sold the loss is incurred by the owners of the firm and not personally by the entrepreneur; the entrepreneur sustains a loss only in proportion to his shareholding. The other shareholders are insuring the entrepreneur's loss. The small loss incurred by the entrepreneur may be likened to the 'excess' on an ordinary insurance claim.

If such losses occurred regularly, however, then the other shareholders might wish to sell out, and the firm would become vulnerable to take-over; alternatively shareholder activists might vote the entrepreneur out of their executive role at an annual meeting (unless the entrepreneur has retained a controlling interest). In effect, the entrepreneur is risking their reputation, and if they lose their reputation then they may lose their livelihood too.

The main reason why people say that entrepreneurship is risky, it seems, is because the entrepreneur's activities appear risky to them. Such assessments of risk are, of course, subjective. They reflect the subjectivity of judgement discussed above. The fundamental sources of risk in an

DOI: 10.1057/9781137305824

innovative business relate to the quality of judgement, and especially to assessments of the size of the market and the probable intensity of competition. Where judgements differ, the entrepreneur who innovates may have undertaken a project that others have rejected because it seemed too risky. The entrepreneur is not necessarily the first person to consider an innovative project, but they may well be the first person to consider it profitable. It is hardly surprising therefore that people who have rejected the project see the entrepreneur as taking risk because on their own assessment of the market the risk in very big indeed.

The idea that entrepreneurs bear risk is attractive to some economists because they are puzzled by the fact that some successful entrepreneurs consistently earn high profits. Entrepreneurship theory suggests that such high profits are a reward for superior decision-making, but conventional economists do not like this explanation because it assumes that people have imperfect information. They prefer an explanation consistent with perfect information, and such an explanation is that high profits represent an equilibrium reward for bearing risk. This line of reasoning implies that entrepreneurs do not merely take risky decisions but carry the full consequences of these decisions themselves: a line of argument that has led some economists to assert that every shareholder is an entrepreneur, whether or not they play any role in executive decision-making. By contrast, entrepreneurship theory sees shareholders as insuring the entrepreneur against the consequences of their mistaken decisions. The shareholders are willing to do this because the consequences would be much worse, on average, if they tried to take the decisions themselves, or asked someone else to take them instead. The shareholders trust the entrepreneur because the entrepreneur has a good reputation, normally owns some shares themselves, and would lose their livelihood if they lost their reputation.

2.3.8   The entrepreneur as project manager

The concept of a project has already been introduced into the analysis of innovation as a passing reference, but it is useful to develop the concept further. A project has both a scale and time dimension. It is often large, in terms of the costs incurred up-front and the stream of revenues that follows later. The time scale is also long: a project may break even (accumulated revenue covers accumulated cost) only after several years, and may need to continue even longer if it is to deliver its expected profit.

DOI: 10.1057/9781137305824

The production and distribution of this book may be considered as a project, and its publisher as an entrepreneur. Bringing a book to market requires editing, printing, binding, advertising, warehousing, order-processing and delivery. In most industries production is a multistage process. Some stages of the process cannot start until others have been completed: for example, printing and binding. Projects can be disrupted by a variety of factors, and a delay at one stage can hold up the entire process. Furthermore, a mistake at a later stage can ruin all the work done at an earlier stage. Thus if stock is damaged by an accident in the ware-house, the printing and binding has to begin all over again. Flexibility can be achieved by building slack into the publication schedule, but this creates financial problems.

Projects are time-consuming. Inputs must be purchased before the output is sold. Sometimes forward sales are possible, as when members of a book club commit in advance to purchasing books, but in general revenues lag behind the costs. This means that the project requires financing. The cost of finance is related to the production cost, period of production between start and finish, and the interest rate on a business loan. The entrepreneur must manage some difficult trade-offs. Prolonging the production schedule, for example, may reduce costs but increase the period of production, so that interest charges saved in one way may be spent in another.

The role of the entrepreneur as project manager emphasises that an entrepreneur requires practical business skills as well as bright ideas. A knowledge of contract law is useful for dealing with out-sourced production (e.g. a publisher who employs an independent printer); and a 'good head for figures' is important in costing production and arranging finance. Social skills are required in liaising with authors, and contacts are important in obtaining endorsements from opinion-leaders in relevant fields.

2.3.9 The entrepreneur as team builder

So far the entrepreneur has been portrayed as an individual, but firms and organisations are often described as entrepreneurial too. Legal responsibility for a decision may often reside with a firm, even though the key decisions are taken by the entrepreneur. A focus on the individual is appropriate, however, in the sense that it is ultimately individuals who take decisions. Even in a committee, each individual decides for

DOI: 10.1057/9781137305824

themselves what to say and how to vote. Committees do not have wills of their own, and neither do firms.

Individuals may well consult with each other, however, and very often consensual decisions will emerge from a dialogue in which no-one is sure exactly who first mooted a decision that was made. Many successful entrepreneurs have operated in partnership with others; indeed, prior to the emergence of the joint-stock enterprise the partnership was a very common form of business organisation, and it remains important today in knowledge-intensive service industries such as medicine, law and accountancy.

A partnership is a useful instrument for combining individual skills. Entrepreneurship is a demanding role, and most people will be better at meeting some demands than others. Partnership allows individuals to team up with people who have complementary skills. People from different backgrounds may well have different information to contribute because of their different life experiences. Differences in place of birth, family background, age, gender and professional qualifications can not only strengthen the knowledge base, but also create tensions where ideas are clarified through discussion and debate.

To select team members an entrepreneur needs good self-knowledge; they need to understand their own limitations, so that they can assess the complementary skills they require. Other people are often the best judge of a person's limitations, and so a successful entrepreneur needs to be able to welcome criticism and learn from it. In building a team it is useful to avoid extremes: too much similarity between members fosters group-think and conformity, but too much diversity can create hostility and impair group performance.

All members of the team may be called upon to offer judgements, that is, to offer opinions with which others might not agree. In this sense all the members may be considered to be entrepreneurs. Not all members need to have equal status, however. Some may be shareholders in the business while others are simply employees. Normally it will be the responsibility of one particular member to determine the composition of the team, and in terms of the previous discussion this person may be identified as 'the entrepreneur'.

2.3.10 The entrepreneur as a generalised arbitrageur

Beginning with a case of simple arbitrage between a shopkeeper and a dealer, the analysis has progressed to the organisation of a supply

DOI: 10.1057/9781137305824

chain for a novel product orchestrated by a team of entrepreneurs and financed by a group of shareholders. The basic principle of coordination set out to begin with still applies to the complex system with which the analysis ends. The only difference is that a wider range of resources has been re-allocated to alternative uses, and that this has been effected through the implementation of a project that lasts a considerable period of time. Customers have switched their demand from a mature product to a novel product, workers have been made redundant in the mature product sector and, through a chain of labour market substitutions, this has released other workers to produce the novel product. Production has been timed so that the different stages of production for the novel product can be carried out in the correct order, and this has required work at each stage to be scheduled appropriately.

These interrelated changes have been initiated by the innovating entrepreneur who formed an executive team, raised funding from shareholders, advertised the jobs and devised the marketing strategy. However, the entrepreneur did not administer the entire process as a central planner would have done in a socialist state. Customers made independent decisions based on offers received from the entrepreneur and his rivals in the mature product sector; in response to customers switching away from them, producers of the mature product laid off their workers, some of whom then took the jobs vacated by workers recruited by the entrepreneur, or moved directly to work for the entrepreneur.

From this perspective innovation is simply a generalised form of arbitrage. Instead of involving a single commodity at a single point of time, it involves a range of commodities over a period of time. Any form of entrepreneurial activity is ultimately arbitrage, because to be of economic relevance it must involve a change in the way that resources are used. Any entrepreneurial process can be decomposed into a vast array of individual acts of arbitrage coordinated partly by the entrepreneur and partly by impersonal market forces acting upon the consumers, workers and shareholders with whom the entrepreneur deals.

By specialising the initiation of this process on entrepreneurs, fewer mistakes will on average be made than if some alternative process were used. This is because responsibility for the process will be taken by individuals who have a reputation for possessing relevant information. Although opinions may differ because of the limited information available, and its dispersal across the population, entrepreneurs will, on

DOI: 10.1057/9781137305824

average, reveal better judgement than others. Although they will commit mistakes, they should commit fewer mistakes than would otherwise be made, and thereby enhance the efficiency of the economy.

Further reading

The classical or canonical writings on the economic theory of entrepreneurship, together with the functions they emphasise, are as follows:

Innovation:

Schumpeter, J. A., trans. R. Opie (1934) *The Theory of Economic Development* (Cambridge, MA: Harvard University Press).

Risk-bearing:

Cantillon, Richard, trans. H. Higgs (1755) *Essaisur la Nature du Commerce en Generale* (London: Macmillan).
Knight, F. H. (1921) *Risk, Uncertainty and Profit* (Boston: Houghton Mifflin).

Coordination:

Hayek, F. A. (1949) *Individualism and Economic Order* (London: Routledge Arbitrage).
Richardson, G. B. (1960) *Information and Investment* (Oxford: Oxford University Press).
Kirzner, I. M. (1973) *Competition and Entrepreneurship* (Chicago: University of Chicago Press).

These theories are synthesised in

Casson, M. (1982) *The Entrepreneur: An Economic Theory* (Oxford: Martin Robertson).

Modern theories that emphasise the role of the entrepreneur as an innovator include:

Audretsch, D. A., and M. C. Keilbach (2006) *Entrepreneurship and Economic Growth* (Oxford: Oxford University Press).
Baumol, W. J. (2003) *Entrepreneurship, Management and the Structure of Pay-offs* (Cambridge, MA: MIT Press).

DOI: 10.1057/9781137305824

For a modern treatment of coordination with an emphasis on the entrepreneur as scientist see

Harper, D. (1995) *Entrepreneurship and the Market Process* (London: Routledge).

The link between entrepreneurship and the firm is explored in

Foss, N.J. and P.G. Klein (2012) *Organizing Entrepreneurial Judgement* (Cambridge: Cambridge University Press)

DOI: 10.1057/9781137305824

3

The Historical Significance of the Entrepreneur

Abstract: *Evidence of entrepreneurship can be seen as early as the medieval period, but most literature in the field concentrates on the nineteenth and twentieth centuries. This chapter presents a more balanced picture of the historical significance of the entrepreneur, showing that entrepreneurs were involved in innovative activities across history and contributed to key economic changes. A variety of terms were used to describe entrepreneurial activities in different periods of history. However this chapter demonstrates that chronological comparisons can aid our understanding of the characteristics of successful entrepreneurs.*

Casson, Mark and Casson, Catherine. *The Entrepreneur in History: From Medieval Merchant to Modern Business Leader.* Basingstoke: Palgrave Macmillan, 2013.
DOI: 10.1057/9781137305824.

DOI: 10.1057/9781137305824

3.1 Problems of historical interpretation

3.1.1 Scope of the investigation

This chapter demonstrates how the concept of entrepreneurship can be used to analyse the historical evolution of the economy, as illustrated by the English economy of 1200–2000. A long period reveals the dynamics of change and indicates the path by which the modern economy has been reached. A national focus is necessary because the geographies of nations vary significantly, and so it is difficult to generalise about the global economy as a whole. England makes a good national case study because it has a long run of relevant records from the beginning of this period.

The general principles governing entrepreneurship apply at all times and in all places, but the ways in which they manifest themselves depend on the institutions in place at the time. Entrepreneurship was defined in the previous chapter in terms of its function, namely the application of judgement to decisions about the use of resources. The entrepreneur is regarded as an individual, but it is recognised that they can work in partnership with other entrepreneurs. This approach is institution-free; it makes no prior assumptions about the context in which the entrepreneur is obliged to operate, but merely requires that they possess some degree of personal freedom.

Popular thinking about entrepreneurship, however, has been strongly influenced by the rise of small business in Western economies since the 1970s. As a result, modern thinking is not always institution-free. Taking the present as a vantage point, and looking for antecedents such as 'the first modern firm' makes for bad history.

3.1.2 Small and large business

Entrepreneurs are often identified today as the owner-managers of small businesses, which they may have founded themselves. The foundation of a business is a one-off event, however, and is different from controlling a business in which big investment decisions have to be made on a regular basis. A small business that is run in a highly entrepreneurial manner is likely to become a big business, and it would be somewhat perverse to say that a big business was not entrepreneurial when its size was simply a symptom of its success. The success of many small businesses in the US, for example, is reflected in the fact that they became large, while the

DOI: 10.1057/9781137305824

failure of many small businesses in Europe is reflected in the fact that they have remained small.

The same point applies to innovation. Operating in a high-technology sector where continuous innovation is necessary for survival is different from operating in a low-technology sector where maintaining tradition and sticking to routine are perfectly adequate for survival. For historical applications, therefore, it is useful to distinguish between high-level and low-level entrepreneurship. High-level entrepreneurs make significant investment decisions which re-allocate resources from existing activities to novel activities, whilst low-level entrepreneurs re-allocate small amounts of resources between existing activities. High-level entrepreneurs run growing businesses producing innovative products while low-level entrepreneurs typically run low-growth small businesses producing standardised products to a traditional design. The two types of entrepreneur are complementary, since high-level entrepreneurs often employ low-level entrepreneurs as subcontractors or franchisees.

3.1.3   Beyond the profit motive

Contemporary popular culture associates entrepreneurship with the pursuit of profit. It is often assumed that greed is the principal motivation of the entrepreneur. Yet many successful entrepreneurs have became notable philanthropists, and some contemporary entrepreneurs freely admit to having more money than they would know what to do with if they spent it all on themselves. Assuming that profit is the only motive makes it impossible to explain why entrepreneurs have established successful consumer cooperatives and worker cooperatives as a means of sharing their profits with others. Neither can the profit motive account for the entrepreneurial success of the founders of major charities that provide medical care, education and social services to millions of underprivileged people.

It is sometimes suggested that all decisions are ultimately selfish, in the sense that someone who shows compassion for someone else is simply seeking to make themselves feel good by a conspicuously sacrificial action. From a practical standpoint, however, it makes no difference whether they are selfish or genuinely compassionate because their behaviour will be the same. It is simplest to assume that people are rational and that their objectives are partly altruistic and partly selfish. Evidence

DOI: 10.1057/9781137305824

presented below suggests that, contrary to contemporary popular culture, altruism has been an important motivator of entrepreneurial activity.

3.2 The division of labour

3.2.1 Division of labour, specialisation and economies of scale

Chapter 2 introduced the concept of coordination, and showed how entrepreneurs can coordinate the economy by intermediating trade. The focus was on the activities of a single entrepreneur. In a market economy with many entrepreneurs the behaviour of the economy will reflect the aggregate impact of all entrepreneurs.

The presence of one entrepreneur can facilitate the activities of other entrepreneurs. Thus if one entrepreneur decides to innovate a novel product made from a rare mineral ore, some other entrepreneur may sink a mine in order to increase the supply of that ore. Chains of production activities emerge in which entrepreneurs buy and sell to other entrepreneurs before the product reaches the final customer. This involves a division of labour in which complex production processes are broken down into simpler components.

The division of labour was first systematically analysed by the Scottish political economist Adam Smith. Smith argued that the division of labour facilitated specialisation. Each person in the production process could focus on a particular task, and as a result they would become more proficient at that task, thereby increasing overall productivity. For example, if the production of a product involved six different tasks, and each task took one day, then it would take one worker six days (a working week) to produce the product. The worker would accumulate experience slowly because each task would only be repeated once a week. But if six workers were employed, and each were specialised on one particular task, then they would repeat their task every day, and so learn six times more quickly. As a result, the time taken might be halved. Thus each worker could produce two items per day, generating an output of 12 items per week. The division of labour within production therefore boosts productivity.

There is a problem, however. To keep each of the specialist workers fully employed requires an weekly output of 12, whilst to keep one

DOI: 10.1057/9781137305824

worker fully employed by themselves requires an weekly output of only one unit. 'The division of labour is limited by the extent of the market' as Smith put it. So how are the 12 units to be sold? The answer is that the market must expand, and with a fixed overall demand this means that the product must be distributed over a wider area. This in turn means that transport costs will rise because distances are greater. Improvements in transport infrastructure are therefore key to advancing the division of labour and achieving productivity growth.

3.2.2   Mechanisation of tasks

The division of labour boosts productivity in other ways. When a task is simplified it becomes easier to mechanise. It may be possible to design a special tool, or set of tools, that each specialist can employ. Skilled artisans have traditionally taken great pride in the tool sets that they use, and have often made them themselves. Mechanisation can involve replacing human power with animal power, steam power or electricity; this leaves the skilled operative to conserve energy and to focus on the control of the machine. The division of labour therefore facilitates the replacement of labour by capital in the form of durable producer goods such as tools and machinery. Capital and labour continue to work together, with labour controlling the use of capital.

Machines are costly to produce and normally pay back their construction costs over several years. Because they speed up prodcution they require an even larger scale of output than before in order to keep them fully utilised. Mechanisation thereby encourages both mass production (high rate of output) and long production run (large lifetime output). Mechanisation changes the skills required by workers. It has often been claimed that mechanisation undermines traditional craftsmanship by de-skilling the production process. This is not always correct, however, because the operation of precision machines such as lathes requires considerable skill. It also overlooks the fact that the construction and maintenance of machinery involves great skill; these skills are often found in the engineering workshops that produce the machines, however, rather than in the workplaces where the machines are operated.

The design of machines requires a combination of imagination, scientific knowledge and practical skill. Machines are often designed along artistic as well as functional lines, so that they not only perform well but look good too. Iconic machines are often revered as works of art, and displayed in museums at the end of their working lives.

DOI: 10.1057/9781137305824

It is sometimes suggested that mechanisation promoted the growth of the factory system. Prior to mechanisation, it is suggested, production took place mainly at home or on the farm. There are four main reasons for bringing machines into a factory, and two of them have nothing to do with mechanisation; to employ an independent supervisor to monitor workers and assure the quality of the finished product, and to bring adjacent stages of production together and so avoid the cost of transporting semi-finished products between different production sites. The other two reasons are to facilitate the maintenance of machinery using a specialist team, and to share access to a common power source such as a water wheel or a steam engine.

Evidence suggests that all these factors have some influence, and that this influence varies according to the industry involved and the nature of the locality: there is evidence of factory production before the machine age, and domestic manufacturing after the machine age, as well as evidence of a switch to factories during the machine age.

3.2.3 The horizontal division of labour

The division of labour can be both vertical and horizontal. The vertical division of labour is exemplified by multistage production along the lines described above. A horizontal division of labour arises when different varieties of the same product are produced. It was noted in Chapter 2 that novel products are often introduced to solve a particular customer problem. There may be more than one solution to the problem, or it may be possible to package and present the problem to the customer in different ways. As a result, customers face a choice between different varieties of product. In many products, such as foodstuffs, variety occurs naturally, for example, different types of meat are available from different animals, with new varieties being engineered as cross-breeds or hybrids. In other cases, such as consumer durables, variety is simply engineered into the product design or fixed by choice of technology.

The horizontal division of labour has a different logic from the vertical division of labour because it thrives on low-volume production. A horizontal division of labour is particularly valuable when different customers have different preferences, as it allows the customer to choose the specific variety best adapted to their needs. On the other hand, the vertical division of labour is effective at driving down production costs and so offering the consumer value for money. The problem is to reconcile these two requirements.

DOI: 10.1057/9781137305824

The answer lies in versatility. Versatility can be built into the machinery or into the product itself. A versatile machine can be adapted to produce different types of product, while a versatile product can serve the needs of a variety of customers. Versatile machines are often designed with detachable accessories, with different accessories being fitted to produce different varieties of product. Versatile products, on the other hand, tend to be multicomponent goods in which all the accessories are factory-fitted and a switching mechanism allows the customer to activate the ones they need. As a result, the consumers of versatile products often use only a small proportion of the features of their product, but as different types of consumers value different features this allows the product to reach a mass market.

3.3   The geography of production and trade

3.3.1   The spatial dimension of production

The division of labour has an important spatial dimension. By separating out the various tasks a division of labour allows different activities to be carried out at different locations. In a vertical division of labour intermediate stages of production receive semi-processed inputs from the previous stage and despatch semi-processed outputs to the next stage. Given that transport costs tend to increase with distance, this means that the both the upstream (previous) stage and the downstream (later) stage exert a pull on the location of the intermediate stage. If transport costs are high then the pull may be very strong, and all the stages may be co-located. They could all be in the same region, or even inside the same factory (as noted above).

Where adjacent stages are located in different factories in the same region an industrial district may emerge with a specialisation in the industry concerned. Independent producers may co-locate in order to share access to specialised resources – both labour and machinery – that are particularly useful to their industry. This concentration may in turn attract machinery builders who wish to be close to their customers in order to understand their requirements, offer after-sales support, and to make it easy to deliver and install the machinery. The concentration may be reinforced if local schools and universities provide specialised training for the industry.

DOI: 10.1057/9781137305824

A spatial division of labour is anchored at one end by the location of customers and at the other end by the location of raw materials or other basic inputs. Customers are often spatially dispersed and this favours locating the final stage of production at a transport hub. Locations of raw materials may be highly concentrated, however, as in case of some minerals which are found only in certain parts of the world. Mineral ores are often located in mountain regions remote from major centres of population, and therefore there is tension between locating production near the mine and locating it near the customer.

Minerals normally need to be refined before they are used, and refining is an energy-intensive process. Furthermore fuels – especially fossil fuels – are costly to transport. As a result, it is often cheaper to bring the mineral to the fuel rather than the other way round. Historically, mineral refining has usually been located near coal deposits rather than at the mine itself. In order to bring in the ore and export the metal, it is desirable for a refinery to have good transport links.

The cheapest way to transport heavy and bulky loads over long distances has always been by sea. Water provides natural buoyancy for heavy cargoes, and wind provides a free (if intermittent) source of power for sailing vessels. The natural location for metal refining is therefore a port with a deep harbour that is served by a range of long-distance shipping routes. The hinterland of the port should contain abundant fuels, which can be brought down to smelters at the port. Metal supplies will be cheaper at the port than elsewhere, and this may attract metal-using industries. Thus a cluster of related industries may develop around the port.

3.3.2   The geography of distribution

The geography of production cannot be considered independently of the geography of distribution. Distribution becomes critically important as the division of labour expands, because an increasing proportion of products are produced in large volumes at locations remote from the customer, and need to be consigned to the customer efficiently. When the division of labour is limited many households are self-sufficient, particularly in rural areas. As the division of labour extends, local markets emerge in which households exchange their surpluses with each other. In a small community where everyone knows each other, trade may be based on barter and credit rather than currency.

DOI: 10.1057/9781137305824

When transport costs fall and the division of labour expands, the range of products externally sourced by each household or community will increase. A town may develop nearby, importing goods from distant locations. The imports may arrive by sea, so it is useful if the town is a port. An inland port on a navigable river may be more convenient than a coastal port as it may be a point of intersection for local roads. In this case a river crossing is useful to connect communities on opposite sides of the river. To exploit its full potential, a town may invest in a bridge to replace a ferry or a ferry to replace a ford.

Rivers become less navigable as they go upstream, and the head of the river, or the limit of navigation, is therefore a strategic location. It is to this point that people in the interior must travel over land in order to benefit from river traffic. The first bridgeable point of a river is also a strategic location; this may coincide with the head of navigation, or may be further downstream. This is the point at which coastal road traffic crosses the natural obstacle created by the river and it is therefore a 'pinch-point' through which cross-river traffic is funnelled.

Ports involve the transfer of passengers and the transhipment of freight from one mode of transport to another. They are therefore useful sites for hotels and cultural amenities, for passengers who are stopping over, and also for processing industries that import raw materials and export finished products. While heavy and bulky products are relatively easy to transport by sea, compact high-value products are much easier to transport over land.

Where distribution centres are concerned, there is considerable potential for competition. There may be several towns along a river, each vying for trade. Each town will tend to have a captive market comprising the villages and settlements nearby, but there will be many villages which are roughly equidistant from different towns. By improving its facilities a town may be able to win trade away from its neighbours. Unlike a production centre with privileged access to fuels, a distribution centre does not necessarily have any key advantage other than its access to the transport network, and this makes competitive threats from other centres intense.

3.3.3   Elite consumption centres

An emphasis on production and distribution should not distract attention for the potential of other locations to attract economic activity.

DOI: 10.1057/9781137305824

There has always been a strong demand for peace and quiet, away from busy, dirty and noisy industrial centres. Cathedrals, monasteries, shrines, royal hunting grounds and gentrified estates are often located away from centres of industry, but because of their attraction for elite professionals and wealthy courtiers they develop as major centres of consumption and then evolve into centres of trade. They are not normally located at natural transport hubs, however. Indeed some abbeys, and many shrines, are in relatively remote locations.

Military considerations are important too. Rocky outcrops on the bends of rivers have always been popular as defensible positions, and as vantage points from which to survey the surrounding area. A castle located on high ground may also be useful as a statement of authority designed to intimidate the local population. Settlements on hills overlooking rivers are therefore advantageous from a military point of view. In some cases the demands of defence and trade can be combined, by having a castle on the hill and a port and trading centre on the river below – a convenient arrangement for provisioning troops.

Military barracks are often located a day's journey from each other to assist in the logistics of military campaigns, and this may require accommodation to be maintained in remote locations. Whether or not the local economy thrives will depend very much on how much the barracks are occupied. The same point applies to other facilities, such as hunting grounds, where infrequent royal visits may be insufficient to sustain a vibrant local economy.

3.4   Integration versus independence in the division of labour

A complex division of labour needs to be coordinated, but it does not necessarily have to be coordinated by a single entrepreneur. Consider a vertical division of labour in which a mineral ore is smelted, the metal is cast into different shapes, which are then fabricated into a metal tool; this tool is then distributed to retail ironmongers, and sold to local tradesmen. Every stage could be in the hands of a different entrepreneur; one owns a mine, the second a smelter, the third an engineering workshop and the fourth an ironmonger's shop. Each entrepreneur trades with other entrepreneurs; for example, the smelter buys ore from the mine owner and sells metal to the engineer. The system can be coordinated

DOI: 10.1057/9781137305824

by market forces. If the costs of existing mines begin to rise as a result of depletion then the price of metal ore increases and new mines will be started up, while some smelters will close down because they cannot pass on the higher price. As a result the supply of ore will increase and demand for it will fall, thereby stabilising the price.

There can be problems, however. The market may not be competitive; for example, existing mine owners may be able to stop new mine owners from entering the industry. The quality of ore may be variable and this may cause problems in the smelting process. Delays caused by strikes and flooding may disrupt smelting, and this may have knock-on effects on later stages of production. Other arrangements may therefore need to be explored.

One solution is vertical integration, in which a single entrepreneur assumes responsibility for the entire chain of activities. The entrepreneur owns a mine, a smelter, a workshop and possibly (though improbably) a chain of ironmonger's shops. In a large industry there may be several integrated businesses, although they may operate independently of each other. Vertical integration was widely pursued in the 1950s and 1960s, and stimulated the growth of some very large firms. These firms often grew by acquisition, by taking over smaller firms that were involved in just one stage of production.

Vertical integration proved inflexible, however. The manager of the smelter did not like being 'locked in' to buying ore from the company's own mine when cheaper ore was available elsewhere, and likewise the manager of the engineering workshop did not like being forced to purchase metal from a particular smelter. In the 1970s and 1980s integration was reversed as operations were split up though 'downsizing' and divestment.

What emerged in many industries was an entrepreneur that owned the product throughout the chain but did not own the facilities in which it was processed. This allowed the owner to control the product flow but to procure production competitively from independent production facilities. In the example above, the entrepreneur would buy the metal ore from the mine, have it smelted by an independent entrepreneur, and consign it to a workshop where an independent engineer would transform it into tools. It might then be distributed as a branded product to an independent ironmonger who would display it alongside other tools belonging to the same brand. These firms became known variously as 'channel leaders', 'supply chain orchestrators' and 'flagship firms'. Over

DOI: 10.1057/9781137305824

the last 30 years they have globalised, and now coordinate world-wide networks of affiliated operations.

Although the channel leader is often hailed as an institutional innovation, it has important historical antecedents, for example, in the 'putting out' system of the textile industry. Textile production is a multistage process. Prior to the factory system, spinning, weaving and dyeing were 'put out' by merchants to independent workers. These merchants bought wool and sold cloth, and owned the product at all stages in between. They checked the quality at every stage in order to avoid the waste of doing further work on defective product. When production was relocated to the factory, the independent spinners and weavers became employees. With everyone assembled in the factory where they could be readily supervised, it was easier for the factory master to own the machinery as well as the product, and to pay the workers for their time (as wage-earners) rather than for their output (as independent entrepreneurs).

The issue of integration versus independence applies to horizontal integration too. A business that sells a range of different products, or different varieties, is described as a conglomerate. Conglomerates can limit competition between the varieties they produce. They can achieve economies in distribution, for example, products consumed by similar types of customer can be marketed together rather than sold separately. They can also coordinate innovation decisions; for example, they may defer the innovation of a product that would compete with an existing product. The benefits to the economy of horizontally integrated conglomerates are generally held to be lower than those of vertically integrated channel leaders, and this is consistent with the fact that, on average, their profitability appears to be lower too.

3.5 The history of innovation: a Schumpeterian perspective

Joseph Schumpeter is one of the few writers to relate entrepreneurship directly to the historical evolution of the economy. According to Schumpeter, radical innovation re-structures the economy by switching resources from mature sectors to novel sectors. Innovations in certain sectors, such as transport and financial services, affect the entire economy because their products are used not only by final consumers but also by other sectors in the economy. 'General purpose' innovations of this kind can influence productivity in all sectors of the economy.

Innovation in one industry can trigger innovations in other industries. The innovation of the railway is a case in point. The principle of a railway is that a locomotive pulls passengers and freight along a track at speed. The system requires a number of elements to work successfully. These include the locomotive's boiler that generates steam, the piston that drives the wheels, and the rails that guide the locomotive and support its pay-load. Early boilers were low-pressure and too large to be mounted on wheels, but improvements (notably the multiflue boiler) made smaller high-pressure boilers possible. A separate condenser and improved valve gear were devised to improve the efficiency of the piston. This was not enough to make railway viable, however. Cast iron rails broke under the weight of a locomotive at speed, and so it was not until the development of the wrought iron rail that the full potential of the railway could be realised.

At any one time there are latent opportunities, or unrealised innovations, that are waiting for some crucial development to make them viable. Entrepreneurs who recognise these critical obstacles to innovation can focus their efforts on resolving them. The key point is to recognise that the obstacle may lie, not in the industry where the product will be marketed but, in an industry where one of the components of the product will be produced. Improvements in marketing may have to await property developments that result in the building of bigger and better retail outlets (e.g. market halls, departments stores and shopping malls); medical advances may have to await discoveries in chemistry which make new pharmaceutical products possible, and the expansion of international trade may have to await advances in finance that make international banking possible. The innovation process may be likened to the completion of jig-saw, in which the picture is complete only once the last piece is in place. Each constituent technology represents a piece in the jig-saw and the role of the innovator is to identify the missing piece, locate it and complete the puzzle.

Table 3.1 sets out a five-fold classification of innovation presented by Schumpeter. Two of his categories – new processes and new products – relate to design and technology, two relate to territorial discoveries – new markets for exports and new sources of supply for agricultural products and raw materials – and the final category relates to institutional innovation. Examples of each category are given for three main periods:

DOI: 10.1057/9781137305824

TABLE 3.1 *Schumpeter's classification of innovations, with examples*

Type of innovation	Medieval 1200–1500	Early modern 1500–1750	Modern 1750–2000
Design and technology: Process	Wind power (windmills, sailing ships with improved rigging) Water power (overshot mill wheel) Bridge-building (wider and taller arches)	Navigation (improved instruments) Ship-building (design and construction of hulls) River improvement (cuts and navigations) Stationary steam power and improved pumps Printing (with movable type) Gunnery	Canals Coal gas Railways and steam locomotives Electrical power and lighting Automobiles Mass production and interchangeable parts Robots
Design and technology: Product	Design of arches and buttresses (cathedral architecture, bridges and castles) Improved die-making for metal products	Printed books Popular fashion textiles (e.g. kerseys) Steel blades	Electrical consumer durables Pharmaceuticals Packaging of perishable goods Poster advertising Personal computers and computer games
Territorial discovery: New export markets	Development of links with France following the Norman Conquest	Muscovy Company; East India Company	Cook's discovery of Australia and its subsequent settlement by British emigrants
Territorial discovery: New sources of supply: raw materials	Access to the Silk Road via Mediterranean trade	Expansion of the spice trade Geological discovery of deep coal-fields Geographical discovery (Newfoundland cod fishery, Hudson's Bay Company's trade in beaver pelts from Canada	Mineral ores from Africa Undersea oil
Institutional innovation: New forms of organisation	The borough and its planned market place Merchant guilds	Chartered joint stock companies Reserve banking Factory system	Branch banking Large bureaucratic corporation Global networks of corporate alliances

DOI: 10.1057/9781137305824

medieval, 1200–1500; early modern, 1500–1750; and modern, 1750–2000. The dates are approximate and, for obvious reasons, the table is indicative only. Nevertheless, it suggests a high degree of continuity in innovation and enterprise, with more innovation in the medieval period than is sometimes believed.

3.6 Innovation and the knowledge base

Innovations draw on different types of knowledge. Table 3.2 identifies three types of knowledge used in Schumpeterian innovation: scientific,

TABLE 3.2   *Three types of knowledge exploited in innovation, and generated by different types of people, with examples*

Type of knowledge	Generated by	Medieval 1200–1500	Early modern 1500–1750	Modern 1750–2000
Scientific	Philosophers, scientists, inventors	Mechanics: gearing and power transmission Load-bearing structures Hydraulics Experimentalism	Quantification Measurement Medicine Explosives	Thermodynamics Phase transitions (gas, water, solid) Chemistry Electricity Genetics Aeronautics Mathematics and mathematical logic
Geographical	Explorers, prospectors	Mapping Weather systems	Surveying Astronomy	Geology Natural history Geographical information systems
Institutional	Lawyers, civil servants	Principles of law Formal hierarchy Written record-keeping Taxation and financial systems Civic government and market regulation	Government by representatives Intellectual property rights: patents etc.	Refinement of electoral systems Copyright, trademarks, brands

DOI: 10.1057/9781137305824

geographical and institutional. Superficially, each type of knowledge could be associated with a particular type of innovation, as shown in Table 3.1, but this would be misleading. It is more accurate to say that any innovation draws on all three types of knowledge to some degree, although the degree to which a given type of knowledge is involved will depend on the type of innovation and the sector concerned.

The occupations and professions listed in the second column relate to the types of individuals with whom entrepreneurs interact in carrying out their innovations. Entrepreneurs draw upon the knowledge that these individuals possess in order to make their innovations succeed; in some cases they may themselves be a member of one of these professions.

Table 3.2 indicates that the evolution of entrepreneurship is related to the accumulation of knowledge in society. Causation runs not only from knowledge to entrepreneurship, but also from entrepreneurship to knowledge. Experience gained with an entrepreneurial project may feed back into the knowledge base. It was noted in Chapter 2 that innovation can be understood as putting hypotheses to the market test. Innovation also puts products to a technological test; thus the pioneering Comet jetliner passed the market test with flying colours, proving extremely popular with passengers, but failed the technological test because it suffered from metal fatigue – a phenomenon not properly recognised at the time it was built.

The input of knowledge to innovation, and the feedback of experience to enrich the knowledge base, suggests that entrepreneurship has considerable cultural significance. It generates evidence that revises and updates the knowledge base. The feedback from innovation to the knowledge base, followed by the input of knowledge to a subsequent innovation, indicates a potential spill-over from one innovation to another, mediated not by an intersectoral linkage, as suggested above, but by the augmentation of the knowledge base itself.

There are several reasons, therefore, for believing that innovations impact not only on individual product markets but on the economy as a whole. They are:

▸ Interindustry linkages, whereby the innovation of product in one sector places increased demands on some other sector that provides components or raw materials, or is involved in distribution of the product;

DOI: 10.1057/9781137305824

▶ Interaction though the knowledge base, whereby experience with one innovation provides information useful to some other innovation in a different sector;

▶ Innovation bottlenecks, whereby delay in developing some particular component in some specific sector holds up innovations in a range of other sectors, which then proceed concurrently once the blockage has been removed.

The removal of bottlenecks suggests that innovations in different sectors may cluster, and that waves of innovation may occur from time to time that revolutionise the economy. A wave of innovations will stimulate structural change. Competition from new products and processes will render old ones obsolete. Resources will shift from mature-product sectors to novel-product sectors. Workers who cannot adapt may become unemployed, whilst workers who quickly acquire new skills will tend to prosper. Population will move from regions that specialise in the old products to regions that specialise in the new ones.

Historical narratives linking innovation to the economy often identify revolutions as the break-points between one period and the next. The best known of these is undoubtedly the Industrial Revolution of 1760, but many other revolutions have been identified too. Table 3.3 identifies nine revolutions that have taken place between 1200 and 2000. More revolutions could easily have been identified; those included satisfy the criteria that they are recognised in mainstream historical surveys, that they are associated with key events at which some sort of structural break occurs, and they divide the period up conveniently into roughly equal intervals. The dating of every revolution is contentious, and in some case dates have been rounded, for convenience, to the end of a century.

3.7   Institutional innovation

The concept of institutional innovation has received relatively little attention compared to technological innovation, but it is very significant for entrepreneurship. When discussed in a business context, it usually refers to changes in the structure and organisation of firms, for example, a switch from family-managed firms to professionally managed firms, or to the formation of cartels and trusts.

DOI: 10.1057/9781137305824

TABLE 3.3   *'Revolutions' as clustered innovations*

Date	Revolution	Effect
1200	Urban Revolution	Foundation and growth of chartered boroughs and market towns.
1300	Credit Revolution	Markets in currencies and bills of exchange.
1400	'Professional revolution'	Status of warriors and priests declines and status of lawyers, merchants, scholars increases. War becomes intermittent rather than continuous.
1540	Reformation / Tudor dynasty / Price revolution	Rise of individualism in business.
1600	Stuart Commercial Revolution	New maritime, military and mining technologies. Proliferation of chartered trading companies. Mercantilist policies to promote export trade.
1689	Financial Revolution / Agricultural Revolution	Parliamentary control of public finances, formation of Bank of England, National debt., etc. Parliamentary enclosures, new farming practices.
1760	Industrial Revolution	Large factories, mass-produced consumer goods, steam power, etc.
1830	Railway Revolution	Faster communication, lower freight transport costs, access to wider markets.
1900	Managerial Revolution	Large multi-plant firms controlled by salaried professional managers.
1976	Global Competition Revolution	Rise of global supply chains controlled by firms with powerful brands, coordinated using telecommunications, and reliant on partnerships with smaller independent producers.

Note: Initial conditions in 1200 were heavily influenced by a preceding 'Manorial Revolution' which established (qualified) free labour and alienable heritable private property in land. Manors normally controlled areas of land equivalent to a parish or a portion of a parish.

In a long-period historical context, however, it is useful to work with a broader concept of institutional innovation which encompasses changes in the institutional environment of the firm. These may result from innovations made by entrepreneurs in other industries, or from innovations outside the business sector altogether, in politics, religion and society. For present purposes it is useful to focus on innovations made by other entrepreneurs, and to defer discussion of external changes until Chapter 5.

Institutional innovation is particularly important because it usually represents 'general purpose' innovation that affects all sectors of the economy. Not all general purpose innovations are institutional, for

DOI: 10.1057/9781137305824

example new transport and communication technologies, but most institutional innovations are general purpose. Institutional innovations are another factor, therefore, in explaining how an innovation can impact on the economy as a whole.

The Urban Revolution of 1200 and the Financial Revolution of 1689 are both good examples of institutional innovation. The first involved a dramatic expansion in the number of local market centres and the second a dramatic expansion in banking and the market for securities.

The Urban Revolution was driven by local landlords who wished to make their land more profitable by switching some of it from agricultural use to commercial use. Commercial development involved taking either an existing settlement or a green-field site and building a range of facilities, including a market square and houses which were designed to be suitable as residences, workshops and retail outlets. The houses were on plots of a standard size, fronting onto the street, but with plenty of room behind for workshops, gardens, poultry-keeping and so on. To attract enterprising merchants and artisans, there was an option for occupiers to purchase the plots – a major innovation in a society that had only recently emerged from vassalage.

Residents of the town acquired political rights. Within certain limits they could manage their own affairs and elect a local mayor and other officials. The privilege of self-government was only available at a price, however; it involved making an annual payment of rent, known as a farm, to the crown. The system was encouraged by the monarch (most notably Edward I) because they could make money out of the system too. The monarch not only controlled the currency, but also the right to trade, and so market towns required a charter, or at least a letter, confirming their rights. Charters were another costly privilege, but they provided a degree of protection against neighbouring towns establishing rival markets.

Markets in small towns typically operated one day a week, and were supplemented by one or two annual fairs. They provided public benefit because customers could choose between competing traders. They could attract merchants from further afield, thereby widening the range of products on offer. There was a strict system of quality control and considerable concern over the integrity of weights and measures, and market authorities made determined efforts to address these issues. Customers, especially those from overseas, needed to feel confident that

DOI: 10.1057/9781137305824

the quality and quantity of the goods that they purchased in England were consistent across English towns. This was especially important for traders who intended to buy goods in one town and sell them in another.

The system of chartered markets was already in place by 1200, but many of the towns to get early charters were adjuncts to abbeys or castles, so that local merchants enjoyed only limited autonomy. Speculative development of green-field sites acquired momentum after 1200, and charters continued be awarded regularly right up to the Black Death in 1348, after which it was evident that the country was over-supplied with markets. Many markets became defunct and have never been revived since. The legacy was profound, however, as the new towns that survived became major centres of trade. Many of these towns were sited at river crossings, as theory predicts and, together with the bridge, the market place was their main strategic asset.

Although superficially different, the Financial Revolution nearly 500 years later was similar in certain respects to the Urban Revolution. It was driven by wealthy people who had the support of the monarch. It involved the provision of new facilities, which in this case included bank offices and buildings, together with coffee houses where speculators exchanged information. It was dedicated to advancing trade – by financing trade (e.g. bankers discounting bills of exchange) and developing trading links (investment in new trading ventures, such as the notorious South Sea Company). It was also an urban phenomenon, with large financial transactions being concentrated in London and a few provincial cities.

3.8   The identification of entrepreneurs

Most accounts of revolutions do not identify individual entrepreneurs in a systematic way. In the context of the Industrial Revolution, for example, the same characters appear in different accounts, but there are no clear criteria by which some are described as entrepreneurs and others are not. Some authors describe them all as entrepreneurs and others do not use the term at all.

Contemporary sources can indicate who was considered to be the initiator or prime mover in various important high-profile projects. The key actors are generally described in a particular way. Table 3.4 lists some

TABLE 3.4   *Some terms potentially designating an entrepreneur*

Term	Context	Example
Explorer	Territorial	Discovery of Spice Islands
Adventurer	Territorial	Canadian fur trader
Prospector	Territorial	Mining for precious metals
Undertaker	Large project	Project with a long lifetime
Projector	Infrastructure project	Canal or river navigation
Promoter	Infrastructure project	Railway line
Improver	Agriculture, property development	Enclosure of open fields, model farming
Merchant	Trade (mainly wholesale)	Marketing commodities by re-sale
Engineer	Construction	Taking overall responsibility for a large construction project

of the terms that have been used at various times to identify people who played an entrepreneurial role.

Key actors are usually credited with some specific achievement, which involves overcoming some obstacle. This obstacle is portrayed as a legacy of the past which is swept away by the entrepreneur; they remove the obstacle from the path of future generations and usher in a new era. Table 3.5 explains the obstacles that appear to have been overcome in each of the revolutions itemised in Table 3.3.

The attribution of innovations can be controversial particularly where questions of priority are concerned. Historical inquiry often undermines claims to priority and pushes dates of discovery back earlier. As a result, some historians prefer to attribute the willingness to innovate to some rather nebulous cultural change. Where the relevant information is clearly missing this is a reasonable approach, although possibly misleading in that the cultural change may have been affected by the perceived success of some unrecorded pioneer.

It is possible to question whether individual attribution is appropriate. Given that knowledge circulates through social networks, it may be inappropriate to single out a particular individual to receive the credit. Entrepreneurial attribution is different from intellectual attribution, however, because an entrepreneur is not just a thinker or writer, but a 'person of action' who implements a project and receives profit from it, and as such should be easier to identify. Attribution of innovation appears to be more common in the modern period than in the medieval period.

DOI: 10.1057/9781137305824

TABLE 3.5   *Obstacles allegedly overcome by entrepreneurs in effecting revolutions*

Revolution	Obstacles overcome
Urban Revolution	Lack of central place for exchange. Weak consumer protection and quality control. Limited facilities for consumers and craft workers. Failure to develop the potential of geographically strategic locations.
Credit Revolution	Limitation of barter. Costs of currency exchange. Risk of highway robbery of coin and bullion.
'Professional Revolution'	Vested interests of monarchy and Papacy.
Reformation / Tudor dynasty / Price revolution	Restrictions on usury, dress, prices of necessities; rigidities imposed by custom.
Stuart Commercial Revolution	Failure to appropriate potential gains from international trade. Failure to encourage high-risk ventures such as deep mining.
Glorious Revolution / Agricultural Revolution	Failure to control public finances properly; inefficient farming practices based on open fields.
Industrial Revolution	Failure to exploit rotary motion in repetitive work. Failure to exploit economies of a centralised power source and opportunities for economical supervision of a large specialised workforce.
Railway Revolution	Limitations of roads and canals (especially during extreme weather). Failure to exploit possibilities of steam locomotion along 'iron roads'.
Managerial Revolution	Loss of economies of scale in small business. Threat of imitation undermines incentive to innovate. Investment decisions too big to be left to inexperienced amateurs.
Global Competition Revolution	Large managerial firms are inflexible: slow to adjust and weak at commercialising inventions. They are over-staffed and vulnerable to emerging foreign competitors.

Economic incentive may be a factor, as the change seems to occur about 1700, when monopolistic chartered companies and industrial patents were becoming increasingly important in mining and manufacturing industries. The cost of patents remained high until the mid-nineteenth century, however, when there was a boom in patenting. Cultural factors may be important too. Attribution may have been fuelled by an enterprise culture that encouraged an individualistic approach to business; nineteenth-century writers such as Samuel Smiles focused heavily on the attribution of inventions to heroic figures. Overall, there are serious limitations to the ability of historians to establish unambiguous links

DOI: 10.1057/9781137305824

TABLE 3.6   *Historical research on entrepreneurship: scope and limitations of primary sources*

Research question	Dates	Sources of information on outcomes	Scope and limitations
Identify revolutions and assess their impact	1000–	Legislation	High status people who actively participated in revolutions are easily identified, but attribution of specific effects to their specific actions is difficult.
	1000–	Chronicles	
	1500–	Histories	
	1750–	Press reports	
Identify specific innovations and assess their impact	1000–	Landscape and building archaeology	Linking specific innovations to specific people is difficult prior to 1750. More generally, priority is often contested.
	1000–1750	Charters, patents and monopolies	
	1750–	Product advertisements	
Identify specific individuals and assess their impact	1000–	Court records (trade offences, deeds, etc.)	Names of entrepreneurs are easy to find but linking them for biographical purposes is difficult. Representative panels of entrepreneurs are difficult to construct.
	1000–	Tax records	
	1500–	Business correspondence (Cely, Paston, etc.)	
	1750	Company archives	

between innovations and revolutions, their economic impacts, and the individuals responsible for them. These limitations are particularly acute in the medieval period, as shown in Table 3.6. A natural way to address these limitations is through case studies, as demonstrated in Chapter 4.

Further reading

For a long-run perspective on economic evolution see

Gough, J. W. (1969) *The Rise of the Entrepreneur* (London: B.T. Batsford).

Jones, E. (1983) *The European Miracle* (Cambridge: Cambridge University Press).

North, D. C. (1981) *Structure and Change in Economic History* (New York: W.W. Norton).

North, D. C. (1990) *Institutions, Institutional Change and Economic Performance* (Cambridge: Cambridge University Press).

Rosenberg, N. and L. E. Bridzell, Jr. (1986) *How the West Grew Rich* (London: I.B.Tauris).

DOI: 10.1057/9781137305824

The classic reference on the division of labour is

Smith, A. (1776) *An Inquiry into the Nature and Causes of the Wealth of Nations* (Glasgow edition) (Oxford: Oxford University Press, 1976) (the quote is from the title of book I, part III).

On innovations and revolutions see

Freeman, C. (1984) *Long Waves in the World Economy* (London: Frances Pinter).
Schumpeter, J. A., trans. R. Opie (1934) *The Theory of Economic Development* (Cambridge, MA: Harvard University Press).
Schumpeter, J. A. (1939) *Business Cycles* (New York: McGraw Hill).

For the Urban Revolution see

Beresford, M. (1967) *New Towns of the Middle Ages: Town Plantation in England, Wales and Gascony* (London: Lutterworth Press).

For the commercialisation of the medieval economy see

Bailey, M. (1998) 'Historiographical Essay: The Commercialisation of the English Economy, 1086–1500', *Journal of Medieval History*, 24 (3), 297–311.
Britnell, R.H. and B. M. S. Campbell (1995) *A Commercialising Economy: England, 1086–c.1300* (Manchester: Manchester University Press).
Davis, N.(ed.) (1958) *Paston Letters* (Oxford: Oxford University Press).
Hanham, A. (ed.) (1975) *Cely Letters, 1472–1488* (Oxford: Oxford University Press).
Hughes, J. F. (2007) 'King John's Tax Innovations – Extortion, Resistance, and the Establishment of the Principle of Taxation by Consent', *Accounting Historians Journal* 34 (2), 75–107.
Liddy, C. D. (2005) *War, Politics and Finance in Late Medieval English Towns: Bristol, York and the Crown, 1350–1400* (Woodbridge: Boydell & Brewer for Royal Historical Society).
Lloyd, T. H. (1977) *The English Wool Trade in the Middle Ages* (Cambridge: Cambridge University Press).

On the early modern period, including the Financial Revolution and the Agricultural Revolution, see

Nef, J. U. (1964) *The Conquest of the Material World* (Chicago: University of Chicago Press).
Zahedieh, N. (2010) *The Capital and the Colonies* (Cambridge: Cambridge University Press).

DOI: 10.1057/9781137305824

Mingay, G. E. (ed.) (1977) *The Agricultural Revolution: Changes in Agriculture, 1650–1880* (London: Adam and Charles Black).

Willan, T. S. (1976) *The Inland Trade: Studies in English Internal Trade in the Sixteenth and Seventeenth Centuries* (Manchester: Manchester University Press).

On the Industrial Revolution and the Modern Period see

Allen, R. E. (2009) *The British Industrial Revolution in Global Perspective* (Cambridge: Cambridge University Press).

Jones, G. G. (2005) *Multinationals and Global Capitalism: From the Nineteenth to the Twenty-first Century* (Oxford: Oxford University Press).

Mokyr, J. (1985) *Economics of the Industrial Revolution* (London: Allen & Unwin).

Moore, K. and D. Lewis (1999) *Birth of the Multinational: 2000 Years of Ancient Business History, from Ashur to Augustus* (Copenhagen: Copenhagen Business School Press).

Tedlow, R. (1990) *New and Improved: The Story of Mass Marketing in America* (New York: Basic Books).

DOI: 10.1057/9781137305824

4
Case Studies:
The Entrepreneur in Context

Abstract: *This chapter presents case studies which illustrate the range of primary and secondary source material available for the study of entrepreneurship and illustrate points made in Chapter 3. These primarily relate to England, where the available evidence is particularly chronologically complete, but international comparisons are also provided. Some case studies focus on a particular episode in an individual's life in which they overcame an obstacle, made a major achievement or attracted particular attention from their contemporaries. Other case studies examine how entrepreneurs reconciled their personal life and business activities.*

Casson, Mark and Casson, Catherine. *The Entrepreneur in History: From Medieval Merchant to Modern Business Leader.* Basingstoke: Palgrave Macmillan, 2013. DOI: 10.1057/9781137305824.

4.1   Introduction

This chapter presents a range of case studies based mainly on secondary literature. It is designed to illustrate the range of source material available. The focus is on links between the entrepreneurs and the businesses that they established and controlled. Some case studies focus exclusively on firms, drawing on business archives, whilst others focus mainly on the individual, drawing on diaries and letters; the case studies selected here make some attempt to combine the two. Prior to the Industrial Revolution, however, it is difficult to obtain personal profiles of individual entrepreneurs, and also attributions of inventions, as explained in Chapter 3. Some of the case studies therefore are necessarily based on rather limited information.

Several of the studies focus on a particular phase of an individual's life which involved something unusual, and attracted the attention of their contemporaries. Some of the studies relate the individual's business life to their personal life, noting similarities and tensions between them. Some commence with the legacy of the entrepreneur and work backwards in time and discover 'how it all began'. Some writers provide a straightforward narrative of events, whilst others offer interpretation; they relate the entrepreneur's behaviour to the social and institutional conditions of the time, therefore providing a context in which the entrepreneur's actions can be understood.

The case studies do not constitute a representative sample of entrepreneurs, and they are certainly not a random sample generated from a known population. Most of the studies relate to England, and are organised chronologically by period, following the precedent set in Chapter 3. The emphasis is on case studies relating to the medieval period, since this is the period most under-presented in previous work. It is also the most difficult to carry out because of the problems relating to the survival of documents, and their transcription and translation from Latin and Anglo-Norman French. A small selection of international cases are presented afterwards. Common themes are identified in the concluding section.

4.2   Medieval England: 1200–1500

Medieval England experienced what many historians now view as a 'proto-industrial' revolution, characterised by an increase in the number

DOI: 10.1057/9781137305824

of locations at which trade occurred, an increase in the number of transactions conducted, the development of institutions for the regulation of
trade and more widespread use of technology. However potential entrepreneurs had to face a number of challenges, including the Great Famine
of 1315–22, the Hundred Years War of 1337–1453 and the Black Death of
1348–9. There were also more recognisable concerns, for example the
need to reconcile religious beliefs with a career in business and trade,
and the pressure to devote time to other activities, especially political
office, which was unsalaried during this period. As the case studies below
demonstrate, some individuals even recognised economic opportunities
in the most adverse of circumstances.

4.2.1 Two London merchants

Dick Whittington: the man and the myth

Richard Whittington was a medieval merchant whose rags to riches tale
has been immortalised in nursery rhymes and Christmas pantomime.
According to these accounts, in the late fourteenth century, Whittington,
accompanied by his cat, arrived in London from the west of England
to seek his fortune. He soon found a junior position in the house of a
London merchant, and was offered the opportunity to contribute to the
cargo of the merchant's ship when it set sail for Africa. His cat was the
only possession that Whittington could offer.

Dispirited about his failure to make money in London, Whittington
then started to leave the city but as he did so the church bells pealed and
seemed to sound 'Turn again Whittington, lord mayor of London' and
so he returned. Meanwhile Whittington's cat had been such a successful
rat catcher in a royal palace in Africa that it was purchased for a huge
amount. When Whittington returned to London he found that the ship
had docked and he was handed a huge sum of money which allowed
him to enter business and then obtain political office.

The nursery rhymes and pantomimes exaggerate the realities
of Whittington's life but it does seem that he was born in the west of
England and made his way to London, where he first appears in the
records in 1379, already contributing money towards a gift for the nobil-
ity of England.

Whittington began his career as a mercer, a business area that generally involved the sale of cloth, silk, linen and spices. He became a supplier of mercery to the royal court under Richard II and, after Richard

DOI: 10.1057/9781137305824

was overthrown, was fortunate enough to find favour with his successor Henry IV. However an involvement in royal finance began to supersede Whittington's mercery activities; he made large loans to Henry IV and Henry V. The organisation of these loans is not always clear, but it is possible that the interest within them was concealed by recording a higher level of loan in the royal accounts than was actually lent. Alternatively the lender may not have made a financial profit but instead have received certain privileges or extra political influence. In Whittington's case it appears to have led to involvement in the wool trade, notably in a role as a customs collector.

A willingness to take a risk by spending the profits from trade, such as by making loans to the crown, rather than by saving the profits, has been identified as an important feature of Whittington's success in business and politics. His involvement as a supplier to the crown helped him to enter mayoral office for the first time, when Richard II appointed him to replace the mayor Adam Bamme, who died in office in July 1397, and he served further terms as mayor in 1406–7 and 1419–20. His legacies as mayor included the development of Blackwell Hall as a cloth market, the introduction of more sustainable methods of fishing in the Thames and improvements in the sale of ale – one of the staple commodities of the middle ages. He may have also encouraged the production of one of the important surviving records of medieval London, the *Liber Albus,* which provides many details about civic administration.

While Whittington was a successful businessman, his fortune seems to have remained at a fairly stable level from c. 1400 to his death in 1423. Philanthropy is actually seen by many to have been his abiding business legacy. In his will Whittington left money to found an alms house for the poor, as well as bequests to prisoners in city gaols and for improvements to civic infrastructure. His fortune therefore benefitted the citizens as a whole.

The distractions of political office

Gilbert Maghfeld was a fourteenth-century London ironmonger whose rise in political influence appears to have come at the expense of his business. His activities are recorded in his surviving account book.

Maghfeld initially ran a reasonably successful business in the 1370s, importing iron and small amounts of wine, furs and spices and exporting grain and cloth. He appears to have had a reasonably broad customer base for his imports. He sold iron to other London merchants, who then

DOI: 10.1057/9781137305824

sold it to artisans for manufacturing purposes, as well as to merchants from Suffolk and Kent. Wine was sold directly to customers, who included the Archbishop of York and the Mayor of London.

Like many of his contemporaries Maghfeld also had political responsibilities, holding a number of royal appointments in the 1380s including guardian of the seas between Berwick and Winchelsea. While political appointments could often help a merchant's business career, providing extra contacts and an opportunity to influence policy, they were also generally unsalaried. Indeed they often involved an investment of time and a financial outlay of money, such as for hospitality, for which office holders were not reimbursed.

In the 1390s Maghfeld seems to have suffered from these disadvantages of political office. In 1392 Richard II suspended London's liberties, which allowed it to manage its own economic and political affairs, and dismissed the civic officials. When the liberties were restored Maghfeld was appointed to the office of sheriff as a replacement for the man dismissed by Richard. Simultaneously Maghfeld's business appears to have entered a period of irreversible decline. This was possibly because of the time and financial commitment in being a sheriff which caused him to neglect his business, and possibly also because the circumstances in which he gained his office may have damaged some of his business networks and therefore his access to credit. At the time of his death Maghfeld was worth less than half of what he had been in his heyday.

4.2.2 The wool trade and the customs

A politically networked merchant: William de la Pole

William de la Pole was a merchant who was particularly innovative in his movement from the wine and wool trades into the world of royal finance during the early to mid-fourteenth century. Pole's operations were based in the port of Hull in the north-east of England, which became a strategically important location when war with Scotland was resumed in 1327.

Pole was an important entrepreneurial figure because he made a transition from a partnership with his brother in the wine trade to heading a syndicate of merchants who financed the king. Indeed contemporaries described him as 'second to no English merchant'. Until the 1320s the English crown had largely funded its wars through loans from Italian bankers but they were increasingly unable to meet royal demands. Pole and his brother Richard, who held royal appointments related to army provisioning, saw the opportunity to fill the gap by providing loans to the crown themselves. They appear to have raised the capital for their loans by informally organising a group of merchants who did not trust the crown's creditworthiness enough to lend to it directly themselves, but who were willing to lend money to the de la Poles.

Preparations in 1336 for war with France saw Pole's greatest, but also riskiest, financial innovation. Wool was to be the main means by which the war was funded and Pole and his associates formed a syndicate with the purpose of organising all of the customs duties that the king expected to receive from the wool. The English Wool Company, of which Pole was joint head, was granted a monopoly on the export of wool and its sale overseas as well as the right to the compulsory purchase of wool on credit. In return the English Wool Company was required to export 20,000 sacks of wool to the Continent and make an advance loan to the Crown of £200,000. The loan would be repaid from revenue from customs duties.

The scheme was innovative because it was the first time that English merchants had engaged in a formal moneylending association that could rival the Italian banks. However the scheme broke down relatively soon amidst accusations of smuggling by many of its members. As joint head, Pole was one of those held responsible by the crown and put on trial in 1341. Although he did subsequently return to royal moneylending, Pole was never permitted the same degree of responsibility, and his connection to the administration of the royal customs in the mid-1340s resulted in a further set of accusations of financial corruption.

Pole's legacy was mixed. On the one hand he set a precedent for the ability of entrepreneurs to advance socially through business activities, as he was the first English merchant to obtain a high military rank through his achievements in finance rather than war. He also showed that the crown could look to its own subjects for large loans, rather than needing to rely on Italian bankers, and demonstrated that these loans could be organised in a systematic manner.

However Pole's trial demonstrated the political as well as financial risks that faced merchants who engaged in royal finance, and seem to have deterred others from following his lead. In particular an attempt to revive a syndicate of merchants in the 1380s failed because those approached were concerned that they might suffer the same fate as Pole.

DOI: 10.1057/9781137305824

Farmers of the customers

Walter Chiriton and John Goldbeter were two men who became involved in the financing of the siege of Calais, which took place in 1346–7 during the Hundred Years War between England and France. Each of the men headed their own organisation with associates. Chiriton and his associates had an arrangement with the crown which allowed them to lease all the customs of English harbours – meaning that they paid a set amount to the crown in return for the customs revenue. In addition they were involved in repaying the loans that foreign allies and English nobles had made to the crown.

Goldbeter, meanwhile, headed a group of York wool merchants upon whom Chiriton and his associates increasingly relied to mitigate some of the risks involved in royal finance. Goldbeter and his associates formed a second layer of financers who helped Chiriton and his associates meet their obligations to repay royal loans. In return they received a proportion of customs revenue and were permitted to export large amounts of wool without paying customs duty. These privileges helped to reduce their operational costs, but it appears that the main money-making strategy for the Goldbeter group was selling to other merchants, at a profit, the right to export wool free of charge.

The activities of Goldbeter and his associates show that enterprising merchants could become involved in royal financing but in a manner that removed some of the risks of defaulting on their obligations, or having the crown default on them. Goldbeter was one of the men who had been involved in the English Wool Company, arranged by William de la Pole, in the 1330s. Although he seems to have been one of the dishonest associates whose actions were to contribute to the company's failure and Pole's trial, he escaped any major repercussions himself.

As Pole managed, at least temporarily, to carve himself a career as a 'quick fix' man for the king, so too did Goldbeter for Chiriton. When Chiriton's group collapsed in 1349, and the king sought to seize all its assets, Goldbeter nearly became caught-up in a second royal financial scandal. He was accused of owing money to the company although this charge was eventually dropped. Goldbeter does not seem to have learnt his lesson from his two narrow escapes from royal legal action, and was involved in a further financial scandal in the 1360s.

Goldbeter, however, was arguably more successful an entrepreneur than Pole or Chiriton as, unlike them, he kept a greater distance between himself and the crown which largely protected him from business failure

DOI: 10.1057/9781137305824

or political disgrace. He also had a second strategy for making money from his venture into royal finance, namely selling-on at a profit the right to export wool for free.

4.2.3   Enterprising clerics

The church was an important landowner in medieval England, and enterprising clerics did everything they could to maximise their returns. This was not just for their own benefit; the profits were also used to finance religious buildings, to minister to the people and ensure that high standards of religious ritual were maintained.

Exploitation of mineral resources

Coal was an increasingly important source of fuel for a variety of manufacturing processes in the late medieval period and, with easy access to the port of Hull, the bishop of Durham's estates were in a particularly fortunate position to supply it. Mining did not provide a very significant source of income for successive bishops but, as other forms of income deteriorated, it provided a useful income supplement.

The bishops developed close links with the local entrepreneurs who leased their mines. Some of the mines were leased out to members of the local gentry, such as Richard Bellasis who had connections to Henry VIII's advisor Cardinal Wolsey, and they often developed further connections with the bishop by holding local administrative positions for him. A second group of men moved from administrative posts with the bishops into the role of lessee of a mine. William Tomlinson, for example, combined a role as bishop's bailiff of Gateshead with that of a farmer of a mine in Whickham during the period 1531 to 1540. The final group who leased mines from the bishops were lower-status tenants of the bishop, some of whom appear to have worked as managers at other local mines and may have been able to make technical improvements, such as to drainage.

While the bishops were largely content to have the mines run on their behalf, they showed judgement regarding the sustainability of the resource. Limits were set on the amount of coal that could be mined both when the mines were run on behalf of the bishop and when they were leased. This may have been to avoid over-exploitation of the resource so that the mines could continue to operate over a long period without supplies being exhausted.

DOI: 10.1057/9781137305824

Bishops of Durham were not as enterprising as might have been expected in exploiting their mines, making little investment in improvements or new coal fields. However they did develop mutually beneficial relationships with a range of more enterprising groups which allowed them to retain the additional source of income during a relatively unstable economic period. For the local gentry, episcopal officials and tenants, meanwhile, leasing mines from the bishop provided at least a limited outlet for entrepreneurial activity that may have complemented and supplemented a broader portfolio of business interests and operations.

Property development in a medieval city

Writing in the twelfth century the chronicler Gerald of Wales described the 'vast superfluity of wealth and possessions' acquired by the monks of Lanthony Priory, Gloucester in the course of their entrepreneurial activities, contrasting this unfavourably with the poverty of their motherhouse Llanthony Priory in Wales. The monks in Gloucester appear to have received an initial endowment of land in the twelfth century and they acquired further land through purchase and gifts during the twelfth and thirteenth century. This accumulation of property largely ended after the thirteenth century, for reasons that are debated.

While the period of property speculation of the Gloucester monks was relatively short-lived, they showed good judgement in the management of their estate. The priory's properties were concentrated in one of the Gloucester suburbs and they appear to have been content to focus on renting cheap, low-quality property. When properties required restoration the priory usually let them at a lower rent on the condition that the tenant undertook necessary repairs. Although this was a relatively risk-free strategy it was ultimately a successful one, as the overall value of Lanthony's portfolio appears to have increased from the eleventh century to the sixteenth. The priory did undertake one key innovation, however, when it decided in the early sixteenth century to clear some of its low-quality housing and replace it with a single high-value house.

Collaboration between the townspeople and the monastic house occurred when it came to administering revenue from property in Gloucester. Robert Cole, a canon of Lanthony Priory, was appointed by the bailiffs of Gloucester in 1455 to survey which properties in Gloucester had an obligation to pay chief rents to the civic authorities. It appears that, having allowed the collection of such rents to slip for a number of years,

DOI: 10.1057/9781137305824

a general decline in population – possibly caused by reduced immigration from the countryside into the town – had motivated Gloucester's civic authorities to pay closer attention to their finances than previously. The rent roll produced by Cole provided the history of properties which owed chief rent, presumably to show a precedent, and also described the properties so that they could be identified again by rent collectors in the future. Cole also illustrated the roll with principal Gloucester landmarks, such as churches and market crosses.

The selection of Cole, an ecclesiastical officer holder rather than a civic one, to complete this survey appears to have been based on his responsibility for the administering and documenting of Lanthony priory's own properties. Relationships between the two groups had not always been so cordial; during the economic and social disruption that followed the Black Death of 1348–9 there had been many disputes between the priory and the civic authorities, each party accusing the other of the illegal seizure or occupation of properties. By 1455 the civic authorities had gained the upperhand in the dispute, and this, combined with financial crisis that posed a threat to the prosperity of all groups in the town, may have provided some encouragement for the collaboration between Cole and the civic authorities.

4.2.4   Fourteenth-century urban improvement

There was intense competition between local towns in medieval England as they vied with their neighbours for a larger share of trade. The facilities of the town were an important factor. Town walls were important not only for defensive purposes, but for regulating access to markets (for which traders paid a toll) and for reasons of prestige. But maintaining the city walls was an expensive business, often requiring the skilled labour of masons, who were amongst the highest paid artisans in a medieval town. Ingenious financial arrangements were sometimes made for the upkeep of the walls. Because of the importance of river trade, many towns were built on riverbanks, and a bridge was therefore useful to improve access to the town for visiting traders and local customers. Bridges across wide rivers required long spans, which demanded high-technology building techniques. Bridges, like walls, were costly to build and maintain. Repairs could be financed by tolls, paid either by traffic passing over the bridge or boats passing beneath it. Sometimes a chantry was provided to encourage gifts from passing

DOI: 10.1057/9781137305824

travellers, and a hermit might be employed to carry out minor repairs. But these sources of finance were often inadequate, and so local entrepreneurs would step in, as they stood to benefit most from maintaining the trade of the town. Sometimes individuals would take responsibility, but in many cases collective action was involved, as in the cases presented below.

Improving the walls

Richard Spynk was a fourteenth-century Norfolk cloth trader and property speculator whose success brought him unwanted attention. He appears to have been born on a rural estate under the lordship of the Bishop of Ely but to have moved to Norwich where he was permitted to become a freeman of the town, meaning that he contributed to its communal obligations and received in return some of its legal and economic advantages. Tax assessments from the 1350s suggest that he was one of Norwich's wealthiest citizens by that point. While Richard was mainly a merchant in the cloth trade, he appears to have retained a connection to his rural birthplace through land ownership there.

Spynk's main enterprising action was his investment in the infrastructure of Norwich, in particular its walls. The improvement of the walls had two implications for the city. First, the advent of the Hundred Years War with France in 1337 meant that there was a heightened concern with defence. Second, cities were becoming increasingly aware of the advantage that walls, with specified entry points, could give to their ability to collect tolls from traders coming into the city. While the civic authorities of Norwich could see these advantages, and sought in 1337 to improve its defences, many of its citizens could not, and indeed left the city to avoid paying taxes to support the improvement of the existing sections of wall and the construction of new ones.

Stepping in to fill the breach, both financial and literal, Spynk initially agreed to lend the civic authorities the necessary money, which they would then repay at a later date. However the long timescale that this might have entailed, coupled with the lack of cooperation by the other citizens, seems to have led Spynk to propose a more innovative method that benefitted both him and the city. He proposed that instead of lending the money he would donate the extra £100 the city required. In return he either requested, or was offered, exemption from all future taxes and a privilege that permitted any merchants travelling into Norwich to trade with Spynk free passage without paying the usual tolls. Spynk therefore

DOI: 10.1057/9781137305824

may have made some of his money back, but there still seems to have been a significant philanthropic aspect to his actions.

Unfortunately for Spynk, however, his generosity was to have less positive legacy for him than it was for Norwich – which remained the second most important town in England into the fifteenth century. Spynk's generosity came to the attention of Thomas de Lisle, the bishop of Ely. Spynk had been born on one of the bishop's estates but his subsequent move to Norwich appears to have enhanced his legal as well as economic status. This may have been fuel for Lisle, who was a litigious person who often seems to have been motivated by a desire for financial gain. In 1346 Spynk accused the bishop's men of stealing and damaging the property he still owned at his birthplace on one of the bishop's estates. In return, Lisle accused Spynk of being of unfree legal status and of tricking the court into granting him freedom inadvertently by recognising his prosecution of his lord. Eventually an out-of-court settlement was reached, in which Spynk had to pay money to the bishop.

Spynk's activities show how an enterprising individual could align their interests with those of their community. However it also shows that in the medieval period risks to entrepreneurs could come from unexpected quarters. Spynk was able to limit some of the risks of his investment in the walls and limit some of Norwich's risks in a period of warfare and economic competition. However, it is unlikely that he realised that his actions would bring him to the attention of the Bishop of Ely.

Building a town bridge

Citizens of fifteenth-century Abingdon were enterprising in their attempts to re-route trade through their town during a period of general economic decline. Abingdon is situated on the river Thames near Oxford in the south-east of England and in the middle ages was a medium-sized market town with an abbey. However its economic success in the period c.1100–c.1400 was affected by competition from markets in downstream Wallingford and upstream Oxford. There were also tensions between the abbot and the townspeople over the administration of town affairs.

Construction of a bridge over the river Thames at Abingdon provided a means to address competition, cement social relations amongst the townspeople and encourage self-government rather than governance by the abbey. Until the construction of the bridge and causeway much of

DOI: 10.1057/9781137305824

the traffic en-route from London to Gloucester had bypassed Abingdon, where the river had to be crossed by an expensive ferry.

Geoffrey Barbour, a local merchant who had made his fortune in Bristol, saw the potential to capture some of this trade and divert the preferred route. He spearheaded the new project and provided the capital to purchase materials and employ workers. In addition, Sir Peter Basils donated stone from his quarries. Construction began in 1416 and was very intensive with 300 men working noisily over the summer.

The finished bridge was presented as a key example of local enterprise, organised and funded by the local residents. In 1421 the scheme was mentioned in parliament:

> whereas the path and road which run from the town of Abingdon to Dorchester in the county of Oxfordshire, over the river Thames... within the bounds of the franchises, of the abbot of Abingdon,... across which river the lieges of our lord the king and his progenitors, when passing that way, have had their carriage... from time immemorial – were recently flooded by rising water to such an extent that none of the lieges of our lord the king could cross there, or carry any such loads there, without danger of losing their lives, goods, chattels and merchandise; until John Huchons and John Britte, and other people of the said town of Abingdon aforesaid, from their own resources, and from the alms of the people living in the surrounding area, built a bridge to cross at the said place called Burford, and another bridge to cross at the said place called Culhamford... May it please the most mighty prince the duke of Bedford, regent of England... to ordain that the said bridges... should always be and remain common bridges, pathways, path and road for anyone passing or wishing to pass that way, whether on horseback or on foot or in some other manner, with any kind of load whatsoever.

Civic pride was such that 40 years later a local ironmonger produced a poem recording the construction of the bridge and describing its influence on the town which was displayed in the hall of St Helen's hospital.

The long-term legacy of the bridge was also recognised in the provisions made for its upkeep. Willows and poplars were planted along the sides of the bridge to provide wood for repairs to the path. The bridge was administered through the Guild of Holy Cross, which had originally been established to fund the roofing of a local church but had evolved into an important institution in the townspeople's bid for self-government. It is likely that lands and property held by the Guild helped to fund the upkeep of the bridge and causeway, as no income was raised by tolls.

DOI: 10.1057/9781137305824

4.2.5   New technology in medieval England: the miller as entrepreneur

Mills were a key form of technology in the medieval period. Windmills and water-mills performed a variety of functions, from turning grain into flour through to softening cloth. Historians of milling have suggested that four different milling sectors were present in medieval England: 'desmesne, tenant, borough and domestic'. In each sector there were opportunities for entrepreneurship. Desmesne mills were part of a lord's estate and may have served the needs of the lord's household. However lords often preferred to receive a rental income from their mills and some were willing to lease them to tenants in exchange for an annual rent. This provided a second opportunity for entrepreneurship. A similar pattern occurred in the borough sector, the third milling sector. Townspeople could operate a town mill themselves, or lease its operation out. The domestic sector involved the milling of grain by hand. Hand-milling was labour-intensive and, while some additional income could be derived by milling for neighbours and money saved by avoiding paying in money or flour for the use of the lord's mill, economies of scale could not be achieved.

The demesne, tenant and borough sectors therefore provided the best opportunities for aspiring medieval entrepreneurs. Lords took the initial risks by providing the start-up capital for grain mills in particular, with the average mill costing £20–£40 to construct and requiring annual repairs on top. The foundation and operation of a mill was therefore a long-term investment, so why did lords decide to invest in them? The first reason may have been that grain mills allowed the lord's agricultural resources to be exploited more effectively than previously. Secondly, the lord could achieve additional income by encouraging, or coercing, his tenants to use his mill and then taking a proportion of the grain that they brought to be ground there. Some accounts of the Peasants' Revolt of 1381 describe how local lords had prevented their tenants from using hand-mills in order to force them to use the demesne mill, and even used the mill-stones from hand-mills to pave the floors of their manor.

Civic authorities were also key start-up investors in milling technology, especially water-mills for fulling cloth. As with the demesne mills it seems that, in order to secure a return on their investment, civic authorities implemented regulations that required members of

DOI: 10.1057/9781137305824

certain professions, notably bakers and fullers, to use the civic mills. In Winchester, for example, the civic authorities made laws prohibiting fullers from bypassing the city fulling mills, as some fullers were choosing to use competing mills, including those in other towns. It is possible that in some cases the fullers may have been taking their cloth to local mills that they had made investments in.

The greatest return on investment in mills, however, seems to have come from leasing them out to tenants. An example of this arrangement can be found in Colchester in 1311 when John Galyngale (of North Mill), the Prior of St Botolph and John Allot (of Middle Mill), the Prior of St Botolph and his farmer John Sacok, (of New Mill and the Mill near Wyke) and the Abbot of St Botolph (of Bourne Mill) were all accused of allowing their millers to use unproved and unsealed measures. This indicates that while some mills were operated directly by the lord, others were let to tenants. For lords the advantage of leasing a mill was that they could pass on some of the burden of maintenance costs to the tenant. In addition they were more likely to retain their milling monopoly if they cooperated with other interested parties, as this would decrease the potential for the creation of competing mills in the area. Lessees were usually involved in the industry to which the mill was connected, with millers and fullers being the main occupations to enter into mill leasing. They also sometimes came from professions, such as carpentry, which could contribute skills to keep the mill in good repair and therefore protect the investment. The leasing process was made attractive to these groups by the willingness of some lords to shoulder some share of the risks in the milling process, for example by offering to reduce the rent if the mill was out of action for any period and allowing the manorial monopoly to remain.

There was a further risk, however, that those leasing mills had to face, that of social stigma. Medieval literature, such as Chaucer's *Canterbury Tales*, often portrayed millers in a negative light, suggesting that they stole grain during the milling process. The administrative material, such as the court case from Colchester cited above, lends some support to this. Involvement in milling could therefore be a sensible business proposition because grain was a staple product, while cloth was a growth industry, and there was therefore a guaranteed customer base. However the dependency of the customers on the mill, especially when hand-mills were banned, could lead to resentment from those who were not able to make the transition from customer to tenant.

DOI: 10.1057/9781137305824

4.3   Early modern England: 1500–1750

4.3.1   Opportunity-seeking in the sixteenth century

The sixteenth century witnessed both political and economic instability, as well as the religious turmoil of the Reformation. Business risks were great, but the opportunities were great as well. It required considerable entrepreneurial skill to survive and prosper in these turbulent times, but there were rich pickings for those who were successful.

Henry VIII rejected the traditional authority of the Pope, dissolved the monasteries and founded his own national church along Protestant lines. This soured relationships with powerful continental leaders, such as Philip II of Spain. English pirates, supported by the crown, preyed on Spanish treasure ships bringing bullion from South America; piracy was a profitable trade, and made fortunes for maritime entrepreneurs like Walter Raleigh and Francis Drake.

Changes to the customs charged on wool, together with the political difficulties on the continent, encouraged the growth of the English wool trade. Instead of exporting wool as before, it was now consigned to local weavers, many of whom were immigrants from continental Europe, and turned into cloth. The cloth was then exported instead of the wool. There was also a growing domestic market for wool, especially for the supply of military uniforms.

The growth of the wool trade provided opportunities for both agricultural landlords and industrialists. Agricultural landlords could convert arable land to pasture by enclosing the open fields traditionally used by local farmers. Industrialists could establish factories to mass-produce cloth, especially when uniforms were ordered to standard designs. Merchants linked the agriculturalists to the industrialists, coordinating domestic trade flows over long distances.

The new factories provided unwelcome competition for traditional weavers, however, whilst enclosure made many agricultural workers redundant and forced them to leave the countryside and seek work in the towns. The factories had one advantage, however, in that they could absorb some of the labour made redundant elsewhere.

The dissolution of the monasteries released a large amount of land which could be re-deployed for business use and general housing. Wealthy entrepreneurs could purchase abbey lands, demolish the buildings and use the stone to build a country house in the latest Tudor style.

DOI: 10.1057/9781137305824

They were unashamedly spending 'new money' earned by 'new men'; but their country estates ensured that their descendants would be gentlemen rather than humble tradesmen.

These new men no longer felt constrained by religious prohibitions on usury, or any stigma associated with the single-minded pursuit of profit. They were ready to embrace the market system, and to accept the harshness of the competitive process. During the early modern period market principles were increasingly applied to finance and to the labour market as well as to the product market. Custom and tradition exerted fewer constraints on entrepreneurs, and impersonal market forces were allowed freer rein. These changes were contested, but proponents of custom and tradition were ultimately on the losing side.

Profiting from land enclosure: a country farmer of the early sixteenth century

John Heritage had a portfolio career as a wool merchant, general trader and money lender during the period 1495–1520. He operated in Moreton in Marsh in Gloucestershire, England and we are fortunate in being able to follow his business interests through local administrative records and a surviving account book.

In 1495 Heritage inherited his family's farm and the responsibility for his four sisters and their marriages. Through his part in the marriage negotiations for his sisters, Heritage was able to strengthen his social and economic ties with other Gloucestershire families who were engaged in farming or business in the local towns. While these efforts followed a pattern that might have been expected of other local merchants, the death of his father, and shortly afterwards his father's landlord, provided Heritage with an unusual economic and social opportunity. Heritage's new landlord was a teenager and, as Heritage himself was in his twenties, the two men seem to have shared a similar desire to innovate farm management. Together the pair permanently enclosed 360 acres of farmland and launched a transition from the cultivation of crops to the pasture of several hundred sheep. In doing so they were entering into the profitable English wool and cloth trade.

Shortly after the enclosure, Heritage's career took another turn when he and his wife, who came from a wool-trading family herself, had the opportunity to move from the countryside into the town of Moreton in Marsh. From there he administered his wool business, which included the sale of wool from his own flocks and the purchasing and sale of

DOI: 10.1057/9781137305824

wool from other local farmers. In making these transactions Heritage may have benefitted from contacts through his wife's family and through the marriage alliances of his sisters. The best quality wool was retained by Heritage to sell in London while the remainder was sold in local Gloucestershire markets or regional fairs. In his surviving account book Heritage kept records of his sales and also of the money that he lent on security of future deliveries of wool.

Heritage does not appear to have made a fortune from the wool trade in the way in which some of his contemporaries did – his transactions were not with the largest wool producers and he does not appear to have made enough profit to develop other assets such as freehold property. However he did make the most of the opportunities that came his way, and in particular made innovations in estate management.

Jack o' Newbury: a sixteenth-century factory master

John Winchcombe was an industrial capitalist of the cloth trade. While many other clothiers operated through a putting-out system in which products were made by workers in their own homes, Winchcombe centralised his cloth production in a single factory, which shared similarities to the factories of the Industrial Revolution. Winchcombe is immortalised in Thomas Deloney's 1597 novel *The pleasant Historie of John Winchcomb, in his younger years called Jack of Newbery, the famous and worthy clothier of England* in which the protagonist is depicted as self-made business man. Although this work may exaggerate Winchcombe's achievements at the expense of other clothiers who developed factories, it indicates that his activities were considered particularly worthy of attention.

The Winchcombe family's involvement in the cloth trade appears to have begun in the late fifteenth century under John Winchcombe I, about whom little is known other than that his activities were based around Newbury, in the south-east of England. His son John Winchcombe II is the likely subject of Deloney's novel and appears to have been at the peak of his career in the 1530s and 1540s. It is unlikely that Winchcombe II was a totally self-man man, therefore, but he was still innovative compared to his predecessors and many of his contemporaries.

The disposal of monastic property after the English Reformation provided Winchcombe with the opportunity to purchase property cheaply for industrial premises. The scale of Winchcombe's operation is difficult to judge exactly, Deloney suggested that he may have employed as many as a thousand workers while subsequent historians have calculated,

DOI: 10.1057/9781137305824

from his recorded outputs of cloth, that his factory may have contained as many as 50 looms. Like his Victorian contemporaries Winchcombe employed women and children in his factories, Deloney describes how women worked carding the wool and the children sorted it.

Winchcombe recognised that moving to a more industrial form of production might cause quality-control issues, as output was higher and there were more workers to supervise. It seems that he was careful to ensure that standards remained high and his cloth was recognised, even overseas, as being of the highest standard. When orders exceeded production capacity Winchcombe appears to have prioritised the production of the highest grades of cloth and the orders of his most important customers, such as the king's minister Thomas Cromwell. This ensured that standards were not compromised and that influential and wealthy customers did not go elsewhere.

Winchcombe can be seen as a pioneer of the factory process that is more often associated with the nineteenth century, and an entrepreneur who showed judgement in how to operate on a large scale while still retaining a reputation for quality.

Entrepreneurial social networking

The Guild of Holy Trinity, Luton was founded in 1474 and lasted until 1548 when its lands and property were confiscated as part of the English Reformation. A key purpose of a guild was to provide a mechanism for praying for the soul of its members after their death. It was this particular function that the founders of the Holy Trinity Guild, Thomas Rotheram the bishop of Lincoln, John Rotheram, the bishop's brother and a key landowner in Luton, and John Lammer, vicar of Luton, appear to have had in mind when they founded the guild.

The foundation of a guild was a relatively common occurrence in the medieval period, when lifespans were relatively short and concern about the afterlife was intense. Members were attracted by the religious function but also by the other opportunities available through guilds – the development of social networks and political influence. Luton was a relatively small town in the south-east of England which, although near London, was not on the key north–south trade route. Unlike many other English towns its citizens lacked the ability to run their own affairs, and were instead under the control of a local lord. Compared to other locations, such as London, therefore, the economic and political influence open to members of the Holy Trinity Guild may have been small.

DOI: 10.1057/9781137305824

Despite these limitations, however, membership of the Guild provided opportunities for enterprising individuals.

Development of long-distance trading relationships was the first secular opportunity for members. Membership of a guild provided a way in which prospective entrepreneurs could meet other traders and establish customers for their products. In addition, while formal mechanisms for contract enforcement were at an early stage, membership of a guild presented a way of identifying suitable business partners. The Holy Trinity Guild accounts show that, while the majority of members came from Luton and the surrounding area, there were members from more distant locations including Canterbury, Coventry, Halifax and London. The presence of these members may have reflected long-distance trade in wool and travel engaged in by wool merchants.

Maintenance of local economic and social ties were the second opportunity provided to members. The Holy Trinity Guild held an annual feast which was open to all members and probably guests also. The records of food purchased for the feast, and arrangements for entertainment, suggests that it provided an opportunity to reinforce bonds between members and to demonstrate the importance of the Guild (and thus its members) to the local community in general.

Connection with the crown was the third secular opportunity provided by a medieval guild such as the Holy Trinity Guild. In addition to praying for the souls of members, the chaplains funded by the guild said prayers for the royal family. In the case of the Holy Trinity Guild this link to the crown was emphasised in the Guild's register, which showed Edward IV and his wife Queen Elizabeth praying before an image of the Trinity.

4.3.2   The expansion of trade and the development of a national banking system

The seventeenth and early eighteenth century witnessed a number of developments which are often said to have laid the foundations for the Industrial Revolution. The English Civil War 1642–51 brought to a head the differences between Catholics and Protestants, and between Royalists (Cavaliers) and Parliamentarians (Roundheads). It was ultimately resolved in favour of the Parliamentarians. In 1689 a Dutchman was appointed to the throne on the understanding that he would follow the decisions of Parliament. In particular, Parliament exercised the right to

DOI: 10.1057/9781137305824

sanction public expenditure and the taxes raised to finance it. Financial arrangements were improved by creating a national bank (the Bank of England) and a national debt (government bonds of small denominations). In the absence of state pensions, holdings of the national debt proved a useful source of income in old age.

State finance was still inadequate, however, because there was no uniform personal income tax: the administrative apparatus to collect it did not exist until 1801. The state still relied on farming out customs and excise taxes for much of its revenue, and the collection of these taxes provided profitable opportunities for entrepreneurs. The entrepreneurs involved have often been criticised for operating state monopolies that inhibited trade rather than encouraged it. But all taxation distorts incentives in some form or another, and in the case of excise taxes it is not so much the tax itself as the application of different tax rates to different commodities that creates the problems. The state did in fact do its best to promote trade by chartering overseas companies, such as the East India Company, although these companies were also established as monopolies. The fact that they were state monopolies does not mean that they faced no competition, however, because there was strenuous competition at the outset from the Dutch – notably in the spice trade – and later from other countries too. Nevertheless monopoly did appear to generate diseconomies, by disguising excessive costs, and so the Company was subsequently reformed.

The chartered trading company as an institutional innovation

Partners in the early chartered trading companies of the seventeenth and eighteenth centuries were as innovative as their nineteenth-century successors in the methods they used to reduce transaction costs. Many of these companies had headquarters in Europe but traded in commodities that were produced in other parts of the world. Partners in the European headquarters needed information from their overseas outposts in order to ensure that they had enough imports from overseas to meet the demand of the European markets, and in order to coordinate the movement of exports to imports.

Salaried managers were a key innovation introduced by chartered companies such as the Hudson's Bay Company. Careful consideration was given to the personal qualities of these individuals, for example they were expected to be experienced negotiators, skilled inspectors of product standards and masters of languages. The responsibilities of an

DOI: 10.1057/9781137305824

overseas manager involved supervising a local workforce, arranging the shipping of the company's goods, representing the company in an official capacity, and often representing their own European government in an unofficial capacity as a diplomat. Managers were expected to regularly communicate with the European headquarters, providing information about conditions on the ground which could be used for economic forecasting.

The delegation of responsibility to managers created risks for the early chartered companies. Even with communication chains in place it was possible that some managers would attempt to defraud the company, for example by retaining products to sell themselves. Incompetence was also a potential risk, for example managers might lose the company a lot of money if they failed to meet company shipping deadlines. In order to motivate their managers and ensure that they did not abuse company resources, companies such as the East India Company offered high rates of pay and provided free accommodation and travel expenses.

Managers were not the only innovations introduced by these companies; they also reduced transaction costs by cutting out middle-men and markets and founding their own factories overseas.

The East India Company

Sir John Banks (1627–99) served as governor of the East India Company during a period when its activities, and those of the crown that granted its monopoly, were in difficulty. His first forays into trade came when he joined a syndicate that supplied food for sailors in the English wars with the Netherlands and France. He then joined a syndicate that operated ships to India, taking advantage of problems within the East India Company in the 1640s and early 1655 and debates over the validity of its royal licence that granted it a monopoly of trade with India.

Banks showed judgement in his business interests. While personally in favour of free trade with India, when it became apparent that the East India Company monopoly was to be revived by a new charter in 1657 he became a shareholder in it, and a director in 1658. However he gradually withdrew from the Company in the 1660s, possibly because of political pressures from supporters of Oliver Cromwell after the Restoration, or because the Company was not performing as well as expected. During that period Banks entered trade in the Eastern Mediterranean and government finance, as well as returning to the field of naval provisioning.

DOI: 10.1057/9781137305824

In 1669 Banks once again re-aligned his interests to the latest economic and political circumstances, investing large amounts once again in the East India Company and quickly returning to a role of director. In 1672 he was elected its governor. This rapid return and rise may have occurred because Banks's pursuit of a range of interests in the 1660s meant that he was relatively unaffected by the financial crisis that occurred in 1672, when the crown was no longer able to honour its debts. He was to serve as a director or governor on a variety of occasions from 1669 until 1685.

One of the key roles performed by Banks was navigating the Company through the debts that it was owed by the crown, and the loans that the crown expected it to provide. Banks was largely prepared to supply any loans requested by the Crown, receiving in return benefits such as an improved royal charter. These arrangements were not without their critics; there were suggestions that the Company was too closely connected to royal finance and too politicised.

Banks appears to have been a fairly astute businessman whose main skill lay in his ability to time his activities to take advantage of favourable political and economic conditions. He lay low when his business connections with supporters of Cromwell might have caused problems and transferred his allegiances from free trade with India to the monopoly of the East India Company and then away from the East India Company when it suited him. He was therefore able to prosper during an unstable political economic situation and by the 1680s was ten times wealthier than he had been in the 1650s.

Women speculators in the South Sea bubble

The Earl of Huntingdon's five daughters and their friend became involved in the stock market at the time of the South Sea Bubble through their position as customers of Hoare's Bank in London. The founder of the bank, Richard Hoare, was the director of the original South Sea Company and he and his sons made a substantial amount of money before the bubble burst.

The motivations for investment varied amongst the Hastings sisters, as they were known, and also between them and their friend Mrs Jane Bonnell. The unmarried Lady Betty Hastings was a regular user of her Hoare's account and her most intensive use occurred during the South Sea Bubble when she made a profit from buying and selling South Sea and Bank of England stock. Although in a comfortable position financially, Lady Betty was largely dependent on income derived from

DOI: 10.1057/9781137305824

her share of family estates and appears to have wished to increase her other sources of income so 'I should have much more money than I now boast'.

However Lady Betty was wealthier than her four half-sisters and the financial decisions of the others were more focused on augmenting a relatively small income. Lady Ann, for example, described how, compared to Betty's income of £3000 a year, she had a fortune of only £2,878 in total, of which she lost £800 in the South Sea Bubble. For Lady Frances, meanwhile, dividend payments from her East India Stock, at £100–£140 a year, appear to have been a fairly significant part of her annual income. Less is known about the activities of Ladies Catherine and Margaret as they were the only two sisters to marry but Margaret appears to have owned some South Sea stock on which she made a small amount of money that she put into other investments.

Mrs Jane Bonnell, a friend of the sisters, also appears to have invested in the stock market in order to supplement her income after she was widowed and her nephew withheld her annual allowance. She borrowed money to invest in South Sea shares but like Lady Anne she made a loss in her South Sea investments, as evidenced when she was forced to apply to a friend for repayment of a loan she had made to their recently deceased brother. In later years she was largely reliant on financial support from her own sister.

Only Ladies Betty and Margaret, who ironically were probably in least need of the money, can be identified as having made profit from the South Sea stock. Lady Betty used some of the additional income to support her charitable activities while Lady Margaret put it into other investments. Ladies Ann and Frances and their friend Mrs Bonnell were less fortunate.

The activities of the Hastings sisters and Mrs Bonnell have been used as a contrast to typical representations of women as cautious investors. Their connection with Hoare's, with its close links to the South Sea Company, may have encouraged the six women to enter into the stock market and also influenced the direction of their investments. Their actions suggest that women were therefore prepared to take a greater degree of risk in their financial affairs than might have been considered. However, guided as they probably were by their bank, the women were perhaps not entirely innovative in their investments, and not all of them exhibited sufficient judgement to make a reasonable income from their investments.

DOI: 10.1057/9781137305824

4.4 The Industrial Revolution and beyond: England 1750–2000

4.4.1 Technology and markets

The Industrial Revolution used to be presented as a purely technological phenomenon. The pioneers were identified as ingenious artisans and craftsmen who solved the practical problems involved in moving from small-scale domestic production to large-scale factory production. The effects of the revolution were sometimes exaggerated by failing to recognise that impacts were often regional rather than national in scope. Early technological advances were focused on a small set of industries, such as textiles, iron-working and pottery that were located in the Midlands and North-West.

Recent literature presents a more nuanced view. Technology was not the only factor. The supply of finance from well-informed investors like the mill-owner Richard Arkwright was also important. So too were natural resources. Access to water influenced the location of many early factories because it was the key source of power, and it remained a key consideration even when steam power took over. The switch to steam made proximity to coalfields an important consideration.

Product demand was also significant. Mass-markets for fashion textiles and decorative household pottery required an affluent middle class. The profits from trade and banking were important, and so too was the expansion of the overseas empire. Although the United States gained independence in 1776 it continued to be a major customer, and was also the major source of cotton used in the textile industry. Higher incomes stimulated a growth of population, and led eventually to substantial emigration to settler economies such as Australia and New Zealand, which further enlarged the export market.

It was therefore the interaction of demand, supply (natural resources) and technology that made innovation possible. It was not just Britain's ingenious inventors, but also its imaginative entrepreneurs, that allowed Britain to take the lead in the Industrial Revolution.

Pioneers in technology and marketing

Matthew Boulton and James Watt of Birmingham were pioneers in both technology and marketing. It the late eighteenth century they entered into partnership to produce stationary steam engines suitable for use in

DOI: 10.1057/9781137305824

mining. Watt largely played the role of the inventor, and Boulton that of the entrepreneur. In Birmingham, Watt found a particularly congenial situation for his scientific pursuits, which encompassed investigation into topics such as the composition of water and the manufacture of scientific instruments. The Lunar Society had already been developed by Boulton and his friends and included men with an interest in medicine as well as engineering. The society met once a month near to the full moon. The different, yet complementary interests, of the members meant that they were able to add new perspectives to each other's research.

Two main risks faced Boulton and Watt in their business. The first was the ability to protect their ideas while profiting from them. The second was how to market their product overseas when it required a degree of technical knowledge to operate. The pair were innovative in their solutions to both problems. In 1800, in order to retain the loyalty of employees who invented or improved items, Boulton and Watt introduced a contract that allowed such employees to receive higher wages. Their motivation was to keep talent within the firm and avoid employees leaving to establish competing firms. In the process of marketing their product overseas the pair also faced risks of outside industrial espionage from the many visitors who came to the factory. At least one overseas mining engineer, pretending to be a visiting noble, gained enough knowledge during his visit to erect a poor-quality version of Watt's engine in Prussia. On other occasions the complexity of the machinery sold posed a potential deterrent to overseas customers. Boulton and Watt sought to overcome this by using agents to promote their engines overseas and by offering to supply additional business advice to their customers. In selling their mint engines for stamping coins, for example, Boulton also offered advice on how a complete mint could be created, even down to the types of buildings required.

Building the Industrial Revolution

The Industrial Revolution provided opportunities for entrepreneurs to construct housing for the workers leaving the countryside to take up new opportunities in the towns and cities. These entrepreneurs were master builders who undertook to erect complete buildings using a workforce drawn from all parts of the construction industry – from carpenters to plumbers to bricklayers. They undertook contract work for others but, increasingly, purchased land and constructed their own properties, which could then be sold or leased to provide an income. The firms run

DOI: 10.1057/9781137305824

by these master builders, as such entrepreneurs were known, replaced the previous system whereby each profession completed its part of the building independently of the other, with little overall direction other from the person who had commissioned the building.

Alexander Copland and Thomas Cubitt were the two entrepreneurs who pioneered this new form of business operation. Copland was commissioned by the English government to construct a series of military barracks in the late eighteenth and early nineteenth centuries. He showed entrepreneurial judgement solving the problem of how to construct buildings in areas that were often geographically remote. To overcome the difficulties in transporting labour and materials, Copland centralised the construction process, employing all the workers directly and purchasing the materials himself. He set up a fully equipped site where construction could occur constantly and there were no delays while new firms or materials arrived. Copland's innovative methods co-ordinated all aspects of the construction process and also reduced costs by creating economies of scale.

Thomas Cubitt also took advantage of the Georgian building boom. Like Copland he recognised that he could complete contracted work more rapidly if he employed a body of workmen from a range of trades permanently and directly, rather than coordinating deadlines with different firms. In order to make this arrangement profitable and justify retaining staff, however, Cubitt needed a steady stream of work. He realised that, rather than just building to contract for other people, he needed to become involved in property speculation himself. Cubitt developed land in Bloomsbury, Belgravia, Pimlico and Clapham in particular – indeed he has been credited by historians with essentially creating the district of Belgravia. Unlike many other Georgian property speculators Cubitt's developments were of a consistently high standard, from the sewers to the roof. The quality of his work was recognised by none other than Queen Victoria, who appointed him to build Osborne House on the Isle of Wright.

4.4.2 Religion and entrepreneurship: good and bad Quakers

The Quakers are a Protestant sect that believe that everyone has the opportunity to relate directly to God through stillness and reflection. They reject the apostolic succession from which the bishops and priests

DOI: 10.1057/9781137305824

of other churches derive their authority. From their foundation in the seventeenth century they dissented, not only from the Roman Catholic church, but also from the established national church – the Church of England. As dissenters, they were excluded from major public offices until the Repeal of the Test Act in 1828.

Being excluded from public offices drove talented Quakers into business, where they played a prominent part in the Industrial Revolution, and in subsequent developments in the mass-marketing of consumer products. Quakers were noted for the strict discipline they maintained over members through their 'meetings' and for their propensity to intermarry. Quaker businessmen enjoyed a high reputation for personal integrity, and their products similarly enjoyed a reputation for quality. It is possible, however, that some entrepreneurs joined the Quakers to advance their business careers rather than out of religious conviction. In the nineteenth century a number of prominent Quaker families lapsed when their traditional religious commitments came into conflict with new opportunities for profit.

Quakers and chocolate: the paternalistic Cadburys

The Quaker Cadbury family were chocolate manufacturers who are best known for their creation of a 'garden' factory and a workers' village for their employees in industrial Birmingham. However they faced two notable challenges to their business in the late nineteenth and early twentieth centuries. The first was competition from other chocolate manufacturers while the second was accusations of involvement in slavery. These issues threatened to undermine the economic and social integrity that the Cadbury's had worked to achieve, and which were important aspects of their Quaker beliefs.

Competition from Swiss chocolatiers, another British Quaker chocolate manufacturer Rowntree's of York, and from the American firm Hershey's all mounted against Cadbury's in the late nineteenth and early twentieth centuries. Swiss chocolatiers had begun to produce a form a chocolate, known as milk chocolate, which had a less bitter taste than other versions and which they were exporting to Britain. British manufacturers were losing sales to this new, sweeter, product and started to experiment to replicate the Continental varieties, whose ingredients were a closely guarded secret. Cadbury's and its main rival Rowntree's decided that in the interests of protecting the British market against foreign competition they should join forces to ensure that

DOI: 10.1057/9781137305824

the prices of their chocolate was at around the same level and that it was sold by shopkeepers at the price set by each firm. The firms still competed amongst themselves to find a chocolate recipe that emulated that of the Swiss, but they united to keep out Continental competition to the best of their abilities while they did so. However both companies faced competition from America, where the Hershey chocolate firm was also searching for a similar recipe. Eventually Cadbury's and Hershey's were to discover the secret of the new, sweeter chocolate almost simultaneously.

While the innovation of informal collaboration with Rowntree's helped the Cadbury's develop their Dairy Milk product, the other key challenge the firm faced undermined the philanthropic reputation of its founders. While much was made of the attractive conditions in which their Birmingham employees lived and worked, at the start of the twentieth century Cadbury's began to face accusations of sourcing their cocoa beans from plantations where slaves were used. This accusation was all the more serious because as Quakers the Cadbury's were against slavery. It does appear that, before accusations were made in public in the British press, members of the firm had already investigated reports that slave labour was being used, illegally, on the plantations which supplied their cocoa beans. They had sought to resolve the issue through the relevant political channels in the counties involved but faced a series of set-backs while doing so. The reputation of the company was only restored when a court hearing ruled that they had not intentionally purchased cocoa that had been harvested by slaves and when testimony from family members showed the actions that the company had undertaken to reform the plantations concerned.

Quakers and guns: an unusual combination

Unlike many other Quaker entrepreneurs, who sought to reconcile their religion with their business practices, the Galton family were unusual in their willingness to disregard the principles of their faith. The Galtons were gun-manufacturers who assembled a finished gun from the different elements that were manufactured separately in individual workshops. Their involvement in this profession caused tensions with their fellow Quakers, who advocated pacifism and believed that the manufacturing of weapons encouraged warfare. Different generations of Galtons took different approaches to tackling this issue. Samuel Galton the elder eventually retired from gun manufacturing in 1795, shortly after

DOI: 10.1057/9781137305824

stricter policies towards Quaker business practices were introduced by the Society of Friends. However his son Samuel John Galton decided to publically defend his business activities, and as a result was barred from Quaker business meetings, although he continued to informally attend Quaker worship. He was not fully restored to the Society of Friends until his shift into the banking profession.

The Galtons, then, were willing to take some social risks in order to run their business. However they were less innovative in their business practices than might have been expected, especially given that Samuel John Galton was a member of the Lunar Society and a contemporary of the industrial entrepreneurs Boulton and Watt. The Galtons, like other Birmingham gun-manufacturers, were slow to introduce the new technology that was developed in America in the late eighteenth and early nineteenth centuries and produced interchangeable parts that could be used on a range of muskets.

The Galtons were somewhat more concerned with competition nearer to home, however, and were at the forefront of the foundation in Birmingham of a proof house for testing the quality and safety of weapons supplied to the government in the late eighteenth century. At the proof house the quality and safety of guns were tested by firing them in controlled conditions. Before the establishment of a government proof house in Birmingham its manufacturers were required to pay to transport their guns for testing in London. The Galtons were less involved, however, in the foundation of the general proof house, which tested all guns and not just those supplied to the government, in 1813.

Under Samuel John Galton and his son Samuel Tertius Galton the Galton family began to engage in a wider range of business interests. It appears that this occurred partly due to pressure to adhere more closely to Quaker principles and partly from Samuel John's connections with the Lunar Society. Capital from the family business allowed Samuel Tertius to diversify into banking in 1804, with brief success. His father Samuel John made investments in the Birmingham canals, attracted by the opportunity to lower his transport costs, as well as in residential and industrial property. While perhaps not as innovative in their business practices as some of their Birmingham contemporaries in other industries, or their American competitors, the risk that the Galtons took in going against Quaker principles helped them to turn a fortune of £1,114 to £3,000,000 in three generations.

DOI: 10.1057/9781137305824

4.4.3 Evolution of modern business methods in the service sector

Making a market in news: the origins of Reuters

Julius Reuter founded what is now one of the leading international news agencies in London in 1851, the same year as the famous Great Exhibition of the Works of Industry of All Nations. Reuter's success appears to have been based on his judgement of the importance of the telegraph, and especially its ability to transport news over large distances and almost immediately.

Reuter was previously involved in banking and bookselling before journalism and it seems likely that these activities provided him with the financial training and capital for his future activities, as well as an appreciation of business news as a commodity in its own right. It is possible that he also gained his appreciation of the electric telegraph from one of the bank's customers, a German mathematics professor who was involved in its development.

To what extent Reuter deliberately advanced in stages to the point to which he could run his own news agency remains unclear, but during his time at the Berlin bookshop he quickly extended the firm's activities into publishing. After quitting in 1848 he then took a job as a journalist in Paris, a job that he again left swiftly in favour of running his own newspaper. When that publication failed in 1849, Reuter was undeterred and instead returned to Germany, which benefitted from greater press freedom than France. He set up his agency in Aachen, a communications hub as it was on the border of Germany, Belgium and the Netherlands, and began to specialise in selling financial news, transmitted by telegraph from France and Berlin. The location of his agency provided him with a range of customers as, for example, he could sell the French and Belgium news to German newspapers and Belgium and German news to the Dutch newspapers. This commercial opportunity was possible because a systematic telegraph system was not yet in place to connect all the areas so that news could be transmitted directly.

Relocation to London followed quickly, possibly because gaps in the Continental telegraph system were being filled, removing the need for someone like Reuter to fill them. Reuter's Continental experience helped him obtain the role of provider of financial information to the London stock exchange. However it was harder for Reuter to enter the market for political and social news, which was largely controlled by the telegraph

DOI: 10.1057/9781137305824

companies themselves. He was only able to extend his services by offering a free trial and by a major coup when he was able to transmit, as it was delivered, an important speech by Napoleon III.

Throughout the 1860s and 1870s Reuter was able to build on these successes to invest in the telegraph lines themselves, especially those that connected with America, and to open up offices in other countries, particularly those that were part of the British Empire. When he retired in 1878 Reuter did so as head of what was considered by his contemporaries to be the world's leading newsagency. Reuter had based his business around a key innovation, the telegraph, and had himself been innovative in his initial focus on business news and on bridging the gaps in the information network. He took risks to enter into the news agency business, including some less successful business ventures, relocations overseas and free trials to encourage subscriptions. However he also had sufficient judgement to enter into new markets, such as America, and use his previous career experience to inform his new career.

A shipping magnate in the Age of Imperialism

The development of international shipping routes was the area in which Lord Inchcape made a major contribution to enterprise. He made two fundamental achievements, firstly, highlighting to the British government the possibility for developing industry in India and secondly, merging two of the major shipping lines, P&O and the British India Steam Navigation Company, into one company that covered all the ports of the British Empire.

During a position with the shipping firm Mackinnon Mackenzie in India from 1874 to 1894 Inchcape developed a significant role as a spokesperson for the shipping trade, and his experience in India influenced his later forays into British politics. Inchcape proposed that the British government should put greater effort into developing India's own industries, especially in coal and textile manufacturing, rather than only seeing India as a customer for British products. He believed that improvements in shipping in the Indian Ocean could expand available markets for the products of Britain and its empire and permit the development of Indian industries that would complement British ones. He had some success in pursing these and related policies on his return to England in 1894, until World War I led to a re-assessment of Britain's empire.

The second significant aspect to Inchcape's career was his management of the merger, in 1914, of the British India Steam Navigation Company

DOI: 10.1057/9781137305824

and the P&O shipping group in a way that the smaller company, BI, became the most influential. Although officially the merger involved P&O purchasing BI, in practice BI became the dominant firm, with many posts in the newly merged company quickly being filled by members of Mackinnon Mackenzie and BI and the interests of BI dictating the overall direction of the company. The merger created a company that had comprehensive coverage of ports across the British empire, and eliminated replication of routes.

Inchcape was far-sighted in reinforcing the firm's shipping routes with investment in the production of the cargo transported, acquiring tea mills, textile mills and coal mines. These investments helped the company to survive when shipping routes were disrupted during World War I.

Women shipowners

Women managing-owners of ships were required to make important legal and financial business decisions, including the nature of the trade that the ship was engaged in and regarding maritime insurance and law. People management skills were a further important part of the role. The managing owner was required to oversee the business operations of the ship on behalf of the other owners. They also needed to select a reliable ship's master and maintain a strong relationship with him because the ship's master was in charge of authorising repair to the ship and, in some cases, selling its cargo. Prior to the advent of telegrams he could be out of contact from the owners for several months at a time and therefore needed to be trusted to act in their best interests.

Women managing-owners were present in a number of English ports in the nineteenth century, including Whitby, Exeter and Weymouth. Women managing-owners sometimes obtained their positions by being the largest individual shareholder in the ship. However in some cases female manager-owners represented a family whose combined shares gave them the largest shareholding. On other occasions the appointment of a female managing-owner may have been a recognition of the important role that many women played in book-keeping behind the scenes.

Mrs Ann Alice Morton of Exeter was one of the women for whom the role of managing-owner became a full-time career. After the death of her shipowner stepfather in 1863 Ann inherited his shares in four ships and quickly sought to increase her holding in each of them in order to

DOI: 10.1057/9781137305824

become the majority shareholder. She soon became managing-owner of the four ships, which operated a route between Exeter and London carrying passengers and mail. Mrs Morton lost her husband around the same time as her stepfather and her motivation for being a managing-owner may have been to provide for her three young children. Other female managing-owners operated ships with a more significant international trading pattern, such as Mrs Jane B. Avery of North Shields, managing-owner of five ships that travelled to India, Singapore and the Mediterranean.

Single women also acted as managing-owners, sometimes to support their extended family. Miss Isabella Sanderson of Amble was one such example. She supported other unmarried siblings and orphaned nieces and nephews through a portfolio of business interests, which included being the managing-owner of three ships and acting as a linen draper, postmistress and grocer. Like some of the other women managing-owners, family connections may have provided Miss Sanderson with an opportunity – the three ships that she operated were all built by her brother and brother-in-law.

The position of managing-owner was a responsible one, as it involving taking actions on behalf of the other part-owners of the ship. A range of administrative and people skills were required to fulfil the post. That women were accepted in the role gives an indication of contemporary perceptions of their business acumen. That a number of women consciously sought to take the position by, for example, purchasing enough shares to be a majority shareholder, shows that they were not risk-adverse in their business interests, as there was always a chance of a ship being lost on a voyage. For many women the role of managing-owner provided an important source of income to support their family.

An artistic entrepreneur

The distinctive textile and wallpaper designs of William Morris are still familiar today, but the process that led to their creation has been the subject of much historical debate. Morris's creation of a home furnishing company is often seen as an accidental by-product of his collaboration with members of the Pre-Raphealite Brotherhood, who Morris engaged to decorate his house. It is often assumed that the revival of medieval imagery in the products was a reflection of a unsophisticated business operation, and that the labour-intensive production techniques and relatively small production runs hindered the business.

DOI: 10.1057/9781137305824

Morris's own account of his life, however, reveals a more nuanced picture. Morris emphasised that his father was a business man and that he himself was working hard to establish a business during the period when he was receiving recognition for his interest in the medieval period and his poetry. Morris stated that on some occasions he made a conscious decision to abide by certain principles even when he recognised that they would not lead to substantial financial success.

Despite Morris's socialist principles, his decision to use labour-intensive production processes meant that the clients of his company, founded in 1861, were from the upper sections of society. This tension between his political beliefs and business interests was also addressed by Morris in his account of his life, where he argued that the advancement of socialist principles would help to foster an environment in which such art would be accessible to all sections of society.

Morris's interest in the medieval period during the height of the Industrial Revolution, and his conflicting judgements over the importance of business success versus political integrity, meant that he often received little credit as any sort of entrepreneurial innovator. However recent scholarship has suggested that Morris should receive credit as an innovator of the concept of the specialist interior design firm, which was able to provide a range of goods from wall paper to textiles and furniture. Morris recognised the importance of a city-centre show room even when many of his designs were influenced by the rural surroundings of his firm. He also increasingly recognised that a limited form of mass-production was necessary alongside the revival of labour-intensive processes such as hand weaving, and Morris and Co. operated a small factory, interestingly near the site of the medieval Merton Priory.

Origins of a modern supermarket chain

Sainsbury's supermarket chain and its founder, the Sainsbury family, are credited with disseminating innovative American self-service practices to the UK market. The family had been engaged in the grocery business from the nineteenth century and had introduced innovative practices into even their earliest stores, including situating shops near railway stations to improve the speed of delivery of produce, and placing them in the centre of rows of buildings, so that premises could be expanded on either side if customer demand justified it. Early stores were based in the London suburbs and the shopping experience was intended to

DOI: 10.1057/9781137305824

attract middle-class customers by replicating that of more expensive and exclusive city-centre stores such as Fortnum and Mason. The Sainsbury's hoped that by presenting an attractive shopping experience closer to home and providing their own bespoke products, customers would choose to shop locally at their stores rather than travelling into the capital.

While the company expanded successfully in the London area in the nineteenth and twentieth centuries, with over a hundred shops in 1920, World War I and World War II presented particular challenges as supplies were diverted or disrupted and rationing was introduced.

The shift to self-service, as opposed to purchasing each type of good from a different counter, was partly introduced by the Sainburys in response to the aftermath of World War II when there was a shortage of labour in general, and a wider range of career paths open to those who were working. Fewer prospective employees were therefore available to serve at shop counters. In addition the middle-class clientele that formed Sainsbury's customer base were no longer employing servants and were doing their own shopping, often around a full-time job. Customers were therefore looking for faster service. Self-service was originally introduced into the shop in Croydon, which had previously been the model for the Fortnam and Mason style retailing approach. Encouraged by its success, in 1955 the firm opened a purpose-built self-service store and gradually existing stores were converted to the new concept and new ones built to accommodate it.

One of the risks of self-service was how to encourage customers, when faced with a multitude of brands competing for their attention, to pick one brand in preference to another. Sainsbury's recognised this and founded their own design studio to control not only the appearance of their stores but also of their own-brand products.

The Sainsbury's exercised good judgment in their response to many of the challenges of the nineteenth and early to mid-twentieth centuries, and remain an established feature on the British high street. However in later years the firm has suffered from the decision to promote members of the Sainsbury family to managerial positions over other equally qualified, or even more qualified, external candidates. Some commentators have suggested that these decisions caused the firm to lose its innovative edge from the 1980s onwards when it faced increasing competition from other supermarket chains.

DOI: 10.1057/9781137305824

4.5   An international perspective

Jewish merchants in the Middle East

The trading activities of medieval Jewish merchants from Cairo are recorded in a series of letters which rested in the *geniza* of the Cairo synagogue, preserved because they contained the name of God. The letters relate to the period 1000 to 1250 and, while there are many gaps, it is possible to use them to recreate many of the overseas trading networks of these merchants. Jewish merchants in Cairo were engaged in trade with Lebanon, Palestine, Syria, Tunisia and India. Previous research into the Geniza merchants, as this group of merchants are usually referred to by historians, has emphasised their trade in luxury goods. However greater attention has recently been paid to their trade in agricultural products.

Geniza merchants benefitted from a relative absence of barriers to entry into the economic system of the medieval Mediterranean. This provided greater flexibility compared to economic systems which were organised through guilds, and meant that Geniza merchants could move between different commodity markets depending on where the highest demand lay. An ability to judge the relative performance of one market compared to another, and the best time at which to switch markets, was therefore a characteristic of the Geniza merchants.

Judgement as to which trade routes to follow was a further entrepreneurial feature of Geniza merchants, for example some locations were best visited at particular times of the year and merchants also planned itineraries that allowed them to visit a range a of locations during a single long-distance trip. During the period 1000 to 1250 changes in trade routes also became necessary when the central Mediterranean became increasingly politically unstable. From c.1100 this instability meant that the Geniza merchants appear to have reduced the size of their trading networks and shifted to a trading pattern of shorter, more frequent journeys.

The merchants of Jewish Cairo are often perceived to have addressed the risks inherent in overseas trade through informal networks based on family and business associations. These informal networks helped support a merchant's family when he was absent abroad, and allowed the more itinerant merchants who travelled beyond Cairo to act for the more stationary ones and vice versa. There were risks in such informal

DOI: 10.1057/9781137305824

connections, however, as letters concerning business arguments between partners attest to.

Adaptability to different markets was a key feature of the Geniza traders. They have been identified by Greif as innovative in their development of social and business networks, while Goldberg argues that, unlike the Italians, they were able to operate successfully in the Mediterranean without needing to employ violence to control trade routes and gain trading privileges.

Enterprising monks in the French property market

Cistercian monks in Burgundy, France, were entrepreneurial in their development of a property portfolio. Monks obtained property in five ways: gifts, pawns, leases, exchanges and purchases. They obtained a range of types of property that could be exploited in a variety of ways, including for agricultural purposes and for raw materials as well as for rents.

Gifts reflected the piety of benefactors who received spiritual rewards in return. For the monks, however, there was a risk attached to gifts as a route to developing a property because they had limited control over the nature or location of the property they received. A small piece of property some distance from the monastery, for example, could have actually been a drain on financial resources rather than a benefit. The monks could exert greater judgement in relation to the other forms of property transaction, however. Pawning served as a form of credit and involved the monks lending the property's owner money and taking the property as security in return. The monks exercised discretion in who to engage in pawning with, usually only making arrangements with wealthy landowners who were using pawning as a means of raising money to go on crusade.

Leasing provided a way for the monks to consolidate their landholdings in situations when people might not have been willing to gift land. Some Cistercian abbies leased land in order to fill gaps in the landholdings they had access to in the vicinity of their house. Gaps in property could also be filled by exchanges and sales, although these were less common. Exchanges were used by the monks to swap unwanted gifts for pieces of more desirable or useful land, again with the overall aim of creating a coherent monastic estate. Purchase was used when the timing of the acquisition was important, for example the need to establish a grange.

DOI: 10.1057/9781137305824

While the relative absence of exchanges and purchases seems unusual, it has been suggested that property transactions served as a means of strengthening lay-monastic bonds as well as consolidating landholders. Social networks and long-term relationships could develop under the gifting, pawning and leasing system while exchanges and purchases were one-off events.

The monks therefore judged the best ways to obtain property in order to develop a consolidated estate and social bonds with their neighbours. They also exercised judgement in what they obtained. Cistercian estates were usually based in rural, rather than urban, environments and the monks were aware of the range of natural resources (pasture, wood and water) that could be exploited from the land and used by the monks or sold on the open market. In order to sell their excess produce the monks needed to transport it to local markets and they therefore sought a second form of property – freedom from tolls. These duties were often required to be paid to local landowners when goods were transported across their lands but by obtaining gifts of freedom from tolls the monks could make substantial savings on transporting their goods, especially animals, to market. A final key type of property was the income derived from those who operated mills, ovens and panned for salt on lands controlled by the Cistercians.

The Cistercians therefore took a degree of risk in accepting property as gifts, but off-set this against judgment in how to exploit the property they received. They were innovative in the range of ways in which they sought to acquire a geographically coherent estate and in how they chose to exploit it. They complemented their landholdings with other property that reduced transport costs and provided a supplementary income.

Medieval brewers of Japan

Brewers are usually considered to have been the least enterprising group in the medieval economy, producing small quantities for sale within their local community. In medieval Europe many brewers were married women, who faced legal limitations on their economic involvement. The ale they produced was a perishable product, which could not be transported over long distances. However in Kyoto, the capital city of medieval Japan, brewers of the fermented rice drink sake played important roles as moneylenders as well as victuallers.

DOI: 10.1057/9781137305824

Various forms of leadership operated in medieval Kyoto but historians generally agree that the dominant leaders were the aristocracy, the religious establishment and the warriors. These 'overlords' played a role in the economy, offering a degree of protection and benefits to groups in return for taxes. From the twelfth to the fourteenth centuries the overlord of the Kyoto brewers was the local monastery, which was replaced by the local warriors from the fourteenth century.

Brewer-moneylenders performed a range of functions in Kyoto – storage of valuables for a fee, collection and payment of taxes for their monastic or military overlords, banking services in which they paid interest on deposits and, of course, loans. Commercial expansion but also economic and political upheaval fuelled demand for their services. Kyoto had been founded as an administrative centre but by the twelfth century it was also an important manufacturing centre, supplying goods to the local administrators based in the city and, increasingly, to peasants from the surrounding countryside. However alongside this growth there were periods of warfare, attacks by peasants and a number of famines, meaning that people often wanted to pay for safe storage of their valuables or needed a loan to tide them over the destruction of their property or loss of trade.

In order to engage in these activities most moneylenders needed cash to lend, and brewing provided a good cash-generating activity as demand was constant. Kyoto had good access to the rice needed and operating costs for a small brewery were relatively low. It is estimated that around 350 brewer-moneylenders were operating in Kyoto by the early fifteenth century, in a city that had a population that varied between 50,000–100,000.

Some interesting information is available on the identity and entrepreneurial characteristics of these brewer-moneylenders. Firstly, while women often brewed alongside managing a household in Europe, in medieval Japan some female brewers also engaged in moneylending alongside their brewing. Secondly, the most successful brewer-moneylenders appear to have been those who tried to operate outside of the overlord system. The Suminokura family avoided direct affiliation with any of the military overlords and thus was able to remain in business during some of the military upheavals of the fifteenth and sixteenth centuries, unlike some other money lenders who accepted roles as tax collectors for military overlords but then fell out of favour in the factional politics of the time.

DOI: 10.1057/9781137305824

The links that the brewer-moneylenders had with the religious and military overlords, combined with their regular interactions with the citizens, meant that they seem to have become increasingly involved in the local political life of Kyoto. It seems that some were also patrons of the arts.

An Italian merchant

Francesco Datini overcame early adversity, the death of nearly all of his family during the plague of 1348, to forge an extremely successful career as an international financier. The key achievement of Datini's career was his establishment of a network of companies controlled by a parent company in Florence. The origins of Datini's business expertise, and the extent to which he neglected other aspects of his life in a hard-hearted pursuit of profit, have been much debated. However a re-evaluation of some of Datini's surviving records has shed some new light on these issues.

Datini appears to have developed an initial taste for business by observing his father, a merchant and guild member, in Prato. While it appears likely that Datini would have followed in his father's footsteps, after he and his brother were orphaned in 1348 the direction of Datini's career was determined by his guardians. They organised for the young Datini to train as a merchant in Florence.

With some experience behind him, one of the first judgements that Datini made himself about his career was to move to Avignon, where the presence of the papal court and the natural convergence of a number of trade routes encouraged commerce and finance. During his time in Avignon Datini seems to have been involved in a number of companies selling metal goods, including armour. Innovatively, mercantile companies in Avignon usually engaged in both retail and wholesale trade. This enabled them to reach a wide range of customers and also, through workshops connected to the retail premises, custom-ise items if desired.

An ability to pick good employees and delegate responsibility to them as managers was a key aspect of Datini's ability to expand his operations to cover a range of locations. Loyal employees, even those who had started off as shop workers, were sometimes promoted to partner. Datini also concerned himself with those employed in manufacturing products for his various companies, using a mix of salaried workers and

DOI: 10.1057/9781137305824

self-employed craftsmen who were contracted to work exclusively for Datini's operations.

In 1378 the papal court left Avignon for Rome and Datini appears to have decided that he too should look for a new business opportunity in a new location, which was to be Florence. He saw the opportunity to use his company in Avignon and contacts in other cities to expand his trading operations. Datini developed one of the first examples of the holding company. He invested in opportunities in Prato, Florence, Genoa, Catalonia and Pisa and retained his investments in Avignon. He served as overall director of the operations, while delegating day-to-day running of the local operations to trusted partners or managers. By linking the different companies together Datini enabled commercial information to be shared between them, providing a competitive advantage. He diversified his risks, for example by engaging in the wool trade, metal working and banking. Between them, Datini's companies traded on a route that ran from London to Beirut.

Upon his death Datini left all of his fortune to the poor of Prato. For someone who had devoted their life to making money, and occasionally engaged in unscrupulous practices to do so (such as tax avoidance), this may seem a strange legacy. It has been suggested that the decision may have been partly connected to Datini's lack of a male heir and also a fear of reprisal in the afterlife for some of his business practices. Such a bequest would have resulted in prayers for Datini's soul.

Property development in California

Henry E. Huntington operated a range of complementary businesses that allowed him to profit from nearly all elements of the expansion of Los Angeles. The gold rush of the 1840s, followed by the expansion of the railroads in the 1870s and 1880s meant that Los Angeles became an increasingly popular location for residential and industrial development. Yet while a vast amount of land existed that could be used to fuel demand, local transport links and power and water supplies were crucial. If suburbs were to be developed then their residents would wish to reach the city centre, while the presence of a single harbour and the arid desert landscape imposed limitations on access to fuel and water.

Huntington was not the only entrepreneur to recognise the potential for the expansion of Los Angeles. He was unusual, however, in possessing the capital and connections to overcome these barriers to development. Huntington had inherited several million dollars' worth of railway stock

DOI: 10.1057/9781137305824

from his uncle, which allowed him to invest in a range of complementary businesses – street railroads, water and electricity companies and real estate. His competitors usually only had enough money to operate a single business with small-scale operations.

Before inheriting his fortune, Huntington had also benefitted from experience as a railway manager, which provided him with training and business connections that he used to establish a street railroad and local trolley network that covered central and suburban Los Angeles. Recognising that good transport links had a big influence on where people chose to live, Huntington then began to develop property in the areas alongside the new transportation network. He formed a company to supply power to the trolley system, the excess power from which was used to supply the new developments. He formed a water company to provide new houses and businesses with this other necessity.

Huntington's capital, both financial and social, allowed him to provide all the key infrastructure requirements of transport, accommodation, power and water. As a result he was able to shape the pattern of urban growth in Los Angeles to a much greater extent than any of his competitors. While this was undoubtedly to his personal profit, historians have argued that Huntington's actions promoted prosperity in Los Angeles to a much greater degree than would otherwise have been possible.

4.6 Conclusions

Looking across the studies, several themes emerge which warrant further investigation.

Entrepreneurship is important to many people because they have little opportunity of getting rich any other way. They may not be talented artists or musicians, or excel in any one particular activity, but they may be good all-rounders. As generalists rather than specialists, they are in a good position to synthesise information from different sources. This is not a quality nurtured or rewarded in school or university education, but it can be rewarded by a career as an entrepreneur. Matthew Boulton was not a particularly inventive scientist, for example, but he carved a successful career for himself by commercialising the inventions of others.

Not everyone wants to get rich; some people may be happy to be artists or musicians and remain poor. Aspiration seems to be an important element in entrepreneurship. Many successful entrepreneurs, like Henry

DOI: 10.1057/9781137305824

Huntingdon, reveal a drive for success early in life. Some may 'sell out' for a gentrified lifestyle once they can afford to do so, but others are driven by relentless ambition, as Schumpeter suggests.

Entrepreneurs may come from any rank of society. In the Middle Ages both church and state had a constant need for additional funds, and although they often resorted to borrowing, this was not a sustainable solution in the long run. Kings and clerics could act as entrepreneurs themselves, or they could farm out money-making activities to private entrepreneurs in return for a regular annual income. Gradually the state acquired greater powers of taxation and this made it less dependent on its own business activities. The church's business activities attracted increasing criticism in the sixteenth century – notably the sale of indulgencies – and in response the church gradually withdrew from business, but remained an important landlord. Church and state both gained respectability by distancing themselves from business, and this opened up more business opportunities for individual entrepreneurs.

Risk-taking offers a short-cut to riches, but it increases the risk of losing everything too, as Chiriton and Goldbeter discovered when farming the customs for Edward III. The systematic application of scientific methods to product and process development, which took off about 1700 in the iron industry, increased set-up costs and consequently increased risks; it led to a growing reliance on external sources of finance during the Industrial Revolution.

Profit is not the only motivation for a successful business. Spynk rebuilt the walls of Norwich partly out of a sense of social obligation and partly to enhance his own status. Whittington ploughed back some of the profits from trade into improving London's infrastructure, and Barbour did the same for Abingdon. These men would also have been thinking about their own salvation, and hoping to improve their prospects after death.

Entrepreneurs can gain information by joining a group, and pool their information by working in partnership with others. Nineteenth-century women shipowners, though competitors in their local ports, worked together successfully in the interests of the local shipping trade as a whole. The same applies to the members of the Luton guild 400 years earlier.

Moral and religious convictions can influence the way a business is run. Morris provided opportunities for aspiring young artists, but stopped short of running his business along Socialist lines. Cadbury's followed Quaker principles in treating their workers well, but treated them so well that their wages absorbed all the profits of the business.

DOI: 10.1057/9781137305824

It is often debated whether entrepreneurship can be taught, or whether it is purely innate. These case studies do not address this issue directly. They show, however, that successful entrepreneurs adapt their strategies to the context in which they are operating, and that contexts are highly specific. Thus John Winchcombe used the opportunities afforded by the dissolution of the monasteries to procure cheap business premises, Kyoto moneylenders exploited a need for storage during periods of civil unrest, and Gloucester's Lanthony Priory put aside its differences with the civic authorities to address the problem of urban decline.

One reason that the theory of entrepreneurship set out in Chapter 2 may appear quite abstract is that the general principles of entrepreneurship are very general because they apply across a wide variety of special circumstances. Successful entrepreneurs often reveal an intuitive understanding of these principles, but their success comes ultimately from knowing how to apply these principles to some specific context with which they are familiar.

Further reading

Introduction

For an insightful discussion of the scope of biography in business history, and for additional references see

Corley, T. A. B. (2006) 'Historical Biographies of Entrepreneurs', in M. Casson, B. Yeung, A. Basu and N. Wadeson (eds) *Oxford Handbook of Entrepreneurship* (Oxford: Oxford University Press), 138–57.

Complementary reference works giving more detail on some of the cases presented above are:

Casson, M. (ed.) (2011) *Markets and Market Institutions* (Cheltenham: Edward Elgar).

Casson, M., and C.Casson, (eds) (2013) *History of Entrepreneurship: Innovation and Risk-taking 1200–2000* (Cheltenham: Edward Elgar).

For other collections of business history case studies see the following; they focus mainly on the Industrial Revolution and the evolution of the modern corporation.

Alon, I. and W. Zhang (2011) *Biographical Dictionary of New Chinese Entrepreneurs and Business Leaders* (Cheltenham: Edward Elgar).

DOI: 10.1057/9781137305824

Hamilton, N. A. (1999) *American Business Leaders: From Colonial Times to the Present*, 2 vols (Santa Barbara: ABC-CLIO).

Jeremy, D. (ed.) (1984) *Dictionary of Business Biography: A Biographical Dictionary of Business Leaders Active in Britain in the Period 1860–1980*, 5 vols (London: Butterworth).

Jeremy, D. and G. Tweedale (eds) (2005) *Business History*, 4 vols. (London: Sage).

Jones, G. G. and R. D. Wadhwani (eds) (2007) *Entrepreneurship and Global Capitalism* (Cheltenham: Edward Elgar).

Livesay, H. C. (ed.) (1995) *Entrepreneurship and the Growth of Firms* (Aldershot: Edward Elgar).

Slaven, A. and S. G. Checkland (eds) (1986–90) *Dictionary of Scottish Business Biography, 1860–1960*, 2 vols. (Aberdeen: Aberdeen University Press).

For a global view of the history of entrepreneurship compiled from national studies see

Landes, D. S., J. Mokyr and W. Baumol (eds) (2010) *The Invention of Enterprise: Entrepreneurship from Ancient Mesopotamia to Modern Times* (Princeton, NJ: Princeton University Press).

Richard Whittington

Barron, C.M. (1969) 'Richard Whittington: The Man Behind the Myth', in A. E. J. Hollaender and William Kellaway (eds), *Studies in London History Presented to Philip Edmund Jones* (London: Hodder and Stoughton), 197–248.

Barron, C. M. (2004) *London in the Later Middle Ages: Government and People 1200–1500* (Oxford: Oxford University Press).

Imray, J. M. (1968) *The Charity of Richard Whittington: A History of the Trust Administered by the Mercers' Company, 1424–1966* (London: Athlone).

Sutton, A. F. (2005) *The Mercery of London: Trade, Goods and People, 1130–1578* (Aldershot: Ashgate).

Sutton, A. F. (2004) 'Whittington, Richard (c.1350–1423)', *Oxford Dictionary of National Biography* (Oxford; Oxford University Press). http://www.oxforddnb.com/view/article/29330,date accessed 20 March 2013.

A transcription in modern English of Whittington's will can be found at Medieval English Towns http://users.trytel.com/~tristan/towns/florilegium/community/cmreli17.html, date accessed 20 March 2013.

DOI: 10.1057/9781137305824

A London merchant of the fourteenth century

James, M. (1956) 'A London Merchant of the Fourteenth Century', *Economic History Review*, New Series, 8, 364–76.

A politically networked merchant: William de la Pole

Fryde, E. B. (1988) *William de la Pole: Merchant and King's Banker* (London and Ronceverte: Hambledon Press).

Harvey, A. S. (1957) *The De La Pole Family of Kingston-upon-Hull* (Beverley: East Yorkshire Record Society).

Horrox, R. (1983) *The De La Poles of Hull* (Beverley: East Yorkshire Local History Society).

Sayles, G. (1931) 'The "English Company" of 1343 and a Merchant's Oath', *Speculum*, 6, 177–205.

Fryde, E. B. (2004) 'Pole, Sir William de la (d. 1366)', Oxford Dictionary of National Biography (Oxford, Oxford University Press) online edn., Jan 2008 http://www.oxforddnb.com/view/article/22460, accessed 20 March 2013.

Fryde, E. B. (1983) 'The Wool Accounts of William de la Pole: A Study of Some Aspects of the English Wool Trade at the Start of the Hundred Years' War', reprinted in E. B. Fryde, *Studies in Medieval Trade and Finance* (London: The Hambledon Press), 3–31.

Farmers of the customs

Fryde, E. B. (1983) 'Some Business Transactions of York Merchants, 1336–1349', reprinted in E. B. Fryde, *Studies in Medieval Trade and Finance* (London: The Hambledon Press), 3–37.

Exploitation of mineral resources

Britnell, R. H. (2012) 'The Coal Industry in the Later Middle Ages: The Bishop of Durham's Estates', in M. Bailey and S. Rigby (eds) *Town and Countryside in the Age of the Black Death: Essays in Honour of John Hatcher* (Brepols: Turnhout), 439–67.

Property development in a medieval city

Baker, N. and R. Holt (2008) *Urban Growth and the Medieval Church: Gloucester and Worcester* (Ashgate: Aldershot).

Holt, R. (1990) 'Gloucester in the Century after the Black Death', in R. Holt and G. Rosser (eds) *The Medieval Town: A Reader in English Urban History 1200-1540* (Longman, London and New York), 141–59.

DOI: 10.1057/9781137305824

Langton, J. (1977) 'Late Medieval Gloucester: Some Data from a Rental of 1455', *Institute of British Geographers*, New Series 2, 259–77.

Stevenson, W. H. (ed.) (1891) *Rental of All the Houses in Gloucester AD 1455 from a Roll in the Possession of the Gloucester compiled by R. Cole* (Gloucester: The Corporation of Gloucester).

Thorpe, Lewis (trans. and ed.) (1978) *Gerald of Wales: The Journey Through Wales and The Description of Wales* (London: Penguin).

Improving the walls

Aberth, J. (1996) *Criminal Churchmen in the Age of Edward III: The Case of Bishop Thomas de Lisle* (Pennsylvania: Penn State Press).

Hudson, W. and J. Cottingham Tingey (eds) (1910) *The Records of the City of Norwich*, vol. 2 (Norwich: Jarrold), 216–25, also available at English Medieval Townshttp://users.trytel.com/~tristan/towns/florilegium/government/gvdef10.html accessed 20 March 2013.

Building a town bridge

Cox, M. (1986) *The Story of Abingdon Part 1* (Abingdon: Leach's).

Cox, M. (1989) *Medieval Abingdon: The Story of Abingdon Part 2* (Abingdon: Leach's).

Ditchfield, P. H. and W. Page (eds) (1924) *The Victoria History of the County of Berkshire* 4 vols., vol. 4 (London: The St Catherine Press).

Harrison, D. (2004) *The Bridges of Medieval England: Transport and Society 400–1800* (Oxford: Oxford University Press).

Masschaele, J. (1993) 'Transport Costs in Medieval England', *Economic History Review*, 2nd Series, 46, 266–79.

Toulmin Smith, L. (ed.) (1964) *Leland's Itinerary in England and Wales*, 5 vols., vol. 5 (London: Centaur Press), 116–18.

The quote is from

Curry, A. (ed.) (2013) 'Henry V: Parliament of December 1421, Text and Translation', in C. Given Wilson, P. Brand, A. Curry, R. E. Horrox, G. Martin, M. Ormrod and J. R. S. Phillips (eds) *The Parliament Rolls of Medieval England*, http://www.sd-editions.com/PROME, accessed on 24 February 2013.

New technology in medieval England: the miller as entrepreneur

Langdon, J. (2004) *Mills in the Medieval Economy: England 1200–1540* (Oxford: Oxford University Press).

Blair, J. and N. Ramsay (eds) (1991) *English Medieval Industries: Craftsmen, Techniques, Products* (London and Rio Grande: Hambledon Press).

DOI: 10.1057/9781137305824

Britnell, R. (1986) *Growth and Decline in Colchester 1300–1525* (Cambridge: Cambridge University Press).

Davis, J. (2012) *Medieval Market Morality: Life, Law and Ethics in the English Marketplace, 1200–1500* (Cambridge: Cambridge University Press).

Hassall, W. O. (1973) *They Saw It Happen, Volume 1, 55BC-1485* (London and Southampton: Camelot Press).

Jeayes, I. H. (ed.) (1921–41) *Court Rolls of the Borough of Colchester* 3 vols, vol. 1 (Colchester: Colchester Borough Council).

Keene, D. (1985) *Survey of Medieval Winchester*, 2 vols, vol. 1 (Oxford: Clarendon Press).

Kowaleski, M. (1995) *Local Markets and Regional Trade in Medieval Exeter* (Cambridge: Cambridge University Press).

Profiting from land enclosure: a country farmer of the early sixteenth century

Dyer, C. (2012) A Country Merchant, 1495–1520: *Trading and Farming at the End of the Middle Ages* (Oxford: Oxford University Press).

Jack o' Newbury: A sixteenth century factory master

Jackson, C. (2008) 'Boom-time Freaks or Heroic Industrial Pioneers? Clothing Entrepreneurs in Sixteenth and Early Seventeenth-century Berkshire', *Textile History*, 39, 145–71.

Peacock, D. (2003) 'The Winchcombe Family and the Woollen Industry in Sixteenth-century Newbury'(unpublished University of Reading PhD thesis).

Entrepreneurial social networking

Barron, C. M. (2004) *London in the Later Middle Ages: Government and People 1200–1500* (Oxford: Oxford University Press).

Krammer, S. (1968) *The English Craft Gilds and the Government: An Examination of the Accepted Theory Regarding the Decay of Craft Gilds*, 2nd. edn. (New York: Columbia University Press).

Lunn, J. (1984) *The Register of the Fraternity of the Holy and Undivided Trinity and the Blessed Virgin Mary in Luton Parish Church 1474–1546* (Dunstable).

McKendrick, S., J. Lowden and K. Doyle (eds) (2011) *Royal Manuscripts: The Genius of Illumination* (London: British Library).

Rosser, G. (1994) 'Going to the Fraternity Feast: Commensality and Social Relations in Late Medieval England', *Journal of British Studies*, 33, 430–46.

DOI: 10.1057/9781137305824

Rosser, G. (1997) 'Crafts, Guilds and the Negotiation of Work in the Medieval Town', *Past and Present*, 154, 3–31.

Tearle, B. (ed.) (2012) *The Accounts of the Guild of the Holy Trinity, Luton 1526-7–1546-7* (Woodbridge: Boydell Press for the Bedfordshire Record Society).

The chartered trading company as an institutional innovation

Carlos, A. M. and S. Nicholas (1988) ' "Giants of an Earlier Capitalism": The Chartered Trading Companies as Modern Multinationals', *Business History Review*, 62, 398–419.

Carlos, A. M. and S. Nicholas (1996) 'Theory and History: Seventeenth-century Joint-stock Chartered Trading Companies', *Journal of Economic History*, 56, 916–24.

Jones, S. R. H. and S. P. Ville (1996) 'Theory and Evidence: Understanding Chartered Trading Companies', *Journal of Economic History*, 56, 925–6.

The East India Company

Coleman, D. C. (1963) *Sir John Banks, Baronet and Businessman: A Study of Business, Politics and Society in Later Stuart England* (Oxford: The Clarendon Press).

Tawney, R. H. (1958) *Business and Politics under James I: Lionel Cranfield as Merchant and Minister* (Cambridge: Cambridge University Press).

Yamamoto, K. (2011) 'Piety, Profit and Public Service in the Financial Revolution', *English Historical Review*, 126, 806–83.

Women speculators in the South Sea bubble

Laurence A. (2006) 'Women Investors, "The Nasty South Sea Affair" and the Rage to Speculate in Early Eighteenth-century England', *Accounting, Business and Financial History*, 16, 245–64.

Laurence, A. (2008) 'The Emergence of a Private Clientele for Banks in the Early Eighteenth Century: Hoare's Bank and Some Women Customers', *Economic History Review*, 61, 565–86.

Pioneers in technology and marketing

Jones, P. M. (2008) 'Industrial Enlightenment in Practice: Visitors to the Soho Manufactory, 1766–1820', *Midland History* 33, 68–96.

Macleod, C. (1999) 'Negotiating the Rewards of Invention: The Shop-floor Inventor in Victorian Britain', *Business History*, 41, 17–36.

DOI: 10.1057/9781137305824

Tann, J. (1978) 'Marketing Methods in the International Steam Engine Market: The Case of Boulton and Watt', *Journal of Economic History*, 38, 363–91.

Tann, J. (2007) 'Watt, James (1736–1819)', *Oxford Dictionary of National Biography*, Oxford University Press, 2004; online edn, May 2007, http://www.oxforddnb.com/view/article/28880, accessed 7 March 2013.

Building the Industrial Revolution

Cooney, E. W. (1955) 'The Origins of Victorian Master Builders', *Economic History Review*, 8, 167–76.

Summerson, J. (1970) *Georgian London*, 2nd. edn. (London: Barrie and Jenkins).

Quakers and chocolate: the paternalistic Cadburys

Cadbury, D. (2011) *Chocolate Wars: From Cadbury to Kraft: 200 Years of Sweet Success and Bitter Rivalry* (London: Harper Press).

Smith, H. V. (2012) 'Elizabeth Taylor Cadbury (1858–1951): Religion, Maternalism and Social Reform in Birmingham, 1888–1914' (University of Birmingham unpublished PhD thesis).

Suburban Birmingham: Spaces & Places, 1880–1960 http://www.suburbanbirmingham.org.uk/ accessed 20 March 2013.

Quakers and Guns: an unusual combination

Smith, B. D. (1967) 'The Galtons of Birmingham: Quaker Gun merchants and Bankers, 1702–1831', *Business History*, 9, 132–50.

Making a market in news: the origins of Reuters

Read, D. (1992) *The Power of News: The History of Reuters* (Oxford: Oxford University Press).

A shipping magnate in the Age of Imperialism

Jones, S. (1989) *Trade and Shipping: Lord Inchcape 1852–1932* (Manchester: Manchester University Press)

Women shipowners

Doe, H. (2009) *Enterprising Women and Shipping in the Nineteenth Century* (Woodbridge: Boydell Press).

An artistic entrepreneur

Briggs, A. (ed.) (1977) *William Morris Selected Writings and Designs* (Harmondsworth: Penguin).

DOI: 10.1057/9781137305824

Harvey, C. and J. Press (1986) 'William Morris and the Marketing of Art', *Business History*, 28, 36–54.

MacCarthy, F. (2009) 'Morris, William (1834–1896)', *Oxford Dictionary of National Biography*, Oxford University Press, 2004; online edn., October 2009 http://www.oxforddnb.com/view/article/19322, date accessed 16 October 2012.

Origins of a modern supermarket chain

Kennedy, C. (2000) *The Merchant Princes: Family, Fortune and Philanthropy: Cadbury, Sainsbury and John Lewis* (London: Hutchinson).

Philips, S. and A. Alexander (2005) 'An Efficient Pursuit? Independent Shopkeepers in 1930s Britain', *Enterprise and Society*, 6, 278–304.

Williams, B. (1994) *The Best Butter in the World: A History of Sainsbury's* (London: Ebury Press).

Jewish merchants in the Middle East

Goldberg, J. (2012) Trade and Institutions in the Medieval Mediterranean: The Geniza Merchants and their Business World (Cambridge: Cambridge University Press).

Edwards, J. and S. Ogilvie (2012) 'Contract Enforcement, Institutions, and Social Capital: The Maghribi Traders Reappraised', *Economic History Review*, 65, 421–44.

Greif, A. (2012) 'The Maghribi Traders: A Reappraisal?', *Economic History Review*, 65, 445–69.

Greif, A. (1989) 'Reputation and Coalitions in Medieval Trade: Evidence on the Maghribi Traders', *Journal of Economic History*, 49, 857–82.

Princeton Geniza Project (2012) http://gravitas.princeton.edu/tg/tt, date accessed 21 September 2012.

Enterprising monks in the French property market

Brittain Bouchard, C. (1991) *Holy Entrepreneurs: Cistercians, Knights and Economic Exchange in Twelfth-Century Burgundy* (Ithaca and London: Cornell University Press).

Bell, A. R. and R. S. Dale (2011) 'The Medieval Pilgrimage Business', *Enterprise and Society*, 12, 601–27.

Birch, D. J. (1992) 'Selling the Saints: Competition Amongst Pilgrimage Centres in the Twelfth Century', *Medieval History*, 2 (2), 20–34.

Ekelund, R. B. Jr., R. F. Hebert and R. D. Tollison (2006) *The Marketplace of Christianity* (Cambridge, MA: MIT Press).

DOI: 10.1057/9781137305824

Ekelund, R. B. Jr., R. D. Tollison, G. M. Anderson, R. F. Hébert and A. B. Davidson (1996) *Sacred Trust: The Medieval Church as an Economic Firm* (Oxford: Oxford University Press).

Medieval brewers of Japan

Gay, S. (2001) *The Moneylenders of Medieval Kyoto* (Honolulu: University of Hawai'i Press).

An Italian merchant

Nigro, G. (ed.) (2010) *Francesco di Marco Datini: The Man the Merchant* (Firenze: Firenze University Press for Fondazione Istituto Internazionale de Storia Economica 'F. Datini').

Origo, I. (1963) *The Merchant of Prato: Daily Life in a Medieval Italian City* (Harmondsworth: Penguin).

Portfolio property development in California

Friedricks, W. B. (1989) 'A Metropolitan Entrepreneur *Par Excellence*: Henry E. Huntington and the Growth of Southern California, 1898–1927', *Business History Review*, 63, 329–55.

DOI: 10.1057/9781137305824

5

The Social Embeddedness of Entrepreneurship

Abstract: *Entrepreneurs often owe their success to other people, they are not just 'self-made'. Social contacts provide the entrepreneur with information, workers and a market for their product. This chapter explores how entrepreneurs acquire and enhance social contacts. It shows that the entrepreneur's customers often have a clear perception of what 'debt' the entrepreneur owes to society in general. The chapter concludes with a restatement of the new research agenda that the book has outlined, emphasising the interdisciplinary perspective that the book has provided.*

Casson, Mark and Casson, Catherine. *The Entrepreneur in History: From Medieval Merchant to Modern Business Leader.* Basingstoke: Palgrave Macmillan, 2013. DOI: 10.1057/9781137305824.

DOI: 10.1057/9781137305824

5.1 Introduction

The entrepreneur is often perceived as an individualist and 'self-made person' whose success owes nothing to other people. But in fact the opposite in true. Entrepreneurs are deeply embedded in the economic system, in which they play a crucial role, and in society too. Entrepreneurs can contribute to the economy only because society, in turn, contributes to them. Successful entrepreneurs often owe it all, not to themselves, but to the society to which they belong.

The entrepreneur was described as a coordinator in Chapter 2. The entrepreneur is the hub of a set of economic linkages which might not otherwise exist. Products produced by the entrepreneur's workers are supplied to the entrepreneur's customers. The workers' wages may, in turn, be funded by the entrepreneur's investors. These linkages are coordinated using contracts. The linkages between workers and customers, and between workers and investors, are intermediated by the entrepreneur or, more precisely, by the firm that they have established for this purpose. The differences between the prices at which the contracts with workers and customers are negotiated provides a profit margin for the entrepreneur and their investors. The entrepreneur's share of this margin rewards the entrepreneur for the information they provide that makes these linkages possible.

But where does this information come from? Much of it comes from other people. Some of it may come from observing them but much of it comes from communicating with them. The idea for a new product may come from observing the difficulty that consumers are encountering with an existing product, but most likely it will come from conversations with them, and from hearing their complaints.

Entrepreneurship often depends on a synthesis of information. It is not sufficient to know that there is a potential demand for a product, it is also necessary to know that it is possible to supply it. An entrepreneur may therefore need to take technical advice before launching a new product. They can employ consultants, or hire a scientist, but they may be able to get advice more quickly and cheaply using their personal social network. The entrepreneur may know someone from school or university, or from a local sports club who possesses the relevant knowledge. Indeed, an entrepreneur with a broad range of social contacts may be able to get all the information needed to identify opportunities by 'leveraging' their social contacts.

DOI: 10.1057/9781137305824

Social contacts are useful, not only in discovering opportunities, but in exploiting them too. When an entrepreneur decides to produce a new product, for example, they may hire workers from amongst people they already know, employing friends and relatives, or relatives of friends, and so on. The entrepreneur can trust people that they already know, and if workers let the entrepreneur down the entrepreneur has a sanction: they can tell the workers' friends (who are the entrepreneur's friends too) about their behaviour, and so damage their status. Social linkages are therefore vital in assuring productivity and product quality.

A similar point applies to investors. It was noted in Chapter 2 that people invest in a firm because of the entrepreneur's reputation. Reputation is a social phenomenon that is sustained by social groups. People who know the entrepreneur at first hand converse with people who do not and their opinion then diffuses; those who learn at second-hand pass the opinion on to others, and so the reputation spreads like ripples from a stone thrown into a pool. The spread of reputation allows an entrepreneur to capitalise on a small initial success by funding a subsequent larger project which may hopefully become a big success.

The same point applies to customers. As explained in Chapter 2, an opportunity to innovate often arises from some problem to which a solution is found. This problem may be generic within a specific group. The members of this group may belong to some club or society where they share information about their common problems. An easy way to promote the product is to attend club meetings or advertise in the club magazine. It may even be possible to arrange a demonstration for the membership. Where no club exists the entrepreneur may form one by creating a user group. This provides an opportunity for users to educate each other in the use of the product, and also a forum for them to feed back complaints to the entrepreneur and participate in testing out improvements in the product.

Society also gives the entrepreneur confidence in the contracts that they make. The rule of law gives the entrepreneur confidence that customers will pay for goods delivered to them, and investors confidence that the entrepreneur will pay them the share of profits that is their due. The law can, however, be costly to enforce, but fortunately society also provides a moral code which encourages people to honour contracts even when they face no legal sanctions. Even if offenders evade the law they may not escape their conscience, which will punish them with guilt. The only reliable way for them to avoid guilt is to be honest in the first place.

DOI: 10.1057/9781137305824

5.2   Social groups

Given that social contacts are useful for both recognition and exploitation of opportunities, entrepreneurs will wish to optimise their use of them. This means gaining access to the groups where the most useful information can be obtained. This is sometimes not so easy as it sounds, as most social groups have exclusion mechanisms. The more valuable the information shared within the group, the stronger the exclusion tends to be.

Sometimes access can be gained simply by paying a membership fee; indeed, some clubs set high membership fees to deliberately exclude poorer people. In other cases entry is by election or competitive examination. It is necessary to find a patron or sponsor, or someone who can provide coaching for the entry test. On the whole exclusion mechanisms work against diversity, encouraging groups to reproduce themselves by electing people acceptable to, and therefore similar to, existing members. Entrepreneurs who target elite groups as sources of information therefore need to prepare the ground by first gaining access to individual members whom they can then employ to facilitate their entry to the group.

Some groups are highly structured, having presidents, elected officers and salaried support staff. Others are very informal. Mothers who wait at the school gate to collect their children are a well-known type of informal group which is very useful in introducing newcomers into a local community. Churches may also be welcoming, although church congregations tend to have an internal status system based around the ritual of worship. Nevertheless, entry to such groups can be useful for recruiting employees or investors for a project.

Some groups are more transparent than others. On close examination many groups are composed of factions that compete within the organisation. Everyone is welcome to the annual meeting to elect officials, but behind the scenes some delegates may have the block vote of a faction.

Some groups claim to represent particular sections of the community. Professional associations are a case in point. In knowledge-based sectors professional associations often play an important role in accrediting practitioners, and have significant disciplinary powers, including the right to stop people practicing. Such powers are usually conferred by a higher authority such as the government. Professional associations regularly lobby governments and politicians over policies affecting their members. Governments often devolve powers to professional associations in

DOI: 10.1057/9781137305824

return for their support in the implementation of government policy. Representative groups that wish to exercise powers devolved by government generally need to demonstrate that they are truly representative, and this means that they are normally required to employ transparent procedures.

Entrepreneurs tend to belong to two main types of association, both of which claim to represent the business community: trade associations and local chambers of commerce. Entrepreneurs may also belong to charitable organisations such as rotary clubs, and social organisations such as masonic lodges and friendly societies.

Trade associations are organised on an industry basis. They generally provide a range of membership services for an inclusive fee. These include lobbying government on policy issues of common concern to members such as tariffs, taxes and subsidies; setting industry standards with which member firms must comply; organising national trade fairs, or arranging for members to share the cost of attending trade fairs organised in other countries; promoting a wholesome image of the industry through public events and publicity; organising training programmes and joint research activities; and providing benchmarking services, where firms submit confidential accounting information which is averaged across the membership so that members can see how their own performance compares with the industry average.

Trade associations tend to be particularly popular with medium-size firms. Large firms often prefer to conduct their own lobbying. Large firms can afford to make substantial donations to political parties, which allows them to approach government ministers directly rather than through official channels. Small firms often cannot afford the membership fees.

Chambers of commerce are organised across different industries on a local basis. They may lobby both local government and national government. Because localities often specialise in particular industries, certain industries may dominate a chamber's activities. In a port town for example, maritime industries such a shipping, shipbuilding and import processing may dictate the chamber's agenda.

Information generally flows two-ways through trade associations and chambers: information on government plans is fed through to the industry, for example, to allow government to consult on forthcoming legislation, while at the same time industry views are fed back to government. These flows of information can, in principle, contribute to the

DOI: 10.1057/9781137305824

coordination of the economy. Some political commentators are suspicious of trade associations and chambers, however. It is often alleged that the information they provide to government is biased, and that discussions within the association facilitate inter-firm collusion. Industry standards may be designed to penalise foreign firms in order to protect the domestic market, and meetings of the association may even be a cover for an illegal price-fixing cartel.

5.3   Social entrepreneurs

Society is simply a group of ordinary people by another name. It is ultimately individuals who act to influence the pursuit of profit, the taking of risk and the provision of poverty relief. Just as entrepreneurs step forward to address customer problems, social activists may step forward to address social problems too.

Activists require similar qualities to entrepreneurs. They need contacts to acquire information to identify social problems, imagination to find a solution, and the ability to found an organisation to implement the solution. Activists may therefore be regarded as social entrepreneurs.

Social entrepreneurs often establish new social groups. As the leaders of these groups, they can influence the basic attitudes and beliefs of members. In other words, the leader can influence the culture of the group, and the culture in turn influences the behaviour of the members of the group. Social entrepreneurs may promote trust by encouraging their members to take an optimistic view of other people's integrity. If people believe that everyone else will act honestly then they may infer that 'honesty is the best policy' for themselves as well. Conversely, if people take a pessimistic view of human nature, and expect other people to cheat, the they may decide to pre-empt them by 'getting in first' and cheating themselves. The beliefs espoused by the leader therefore become self-fulfilling.

Leaders sometimes promote the idea that only fellow members of their group can be trusted; they may suggest that non-members cannot be trusted and should even be regarded with suspicion or hostility. While engineering trust is good for the economy, engineering suspicion is bad because it means that economic activity will tend to be concentrated within specific groups. When groups are inward-looking, members tend to disregard the opinions of other groups. This provides an opportunity for economic entrepreneurs to join different groups that are mutually suspicious of each other and identify profit opportunities by arbitraging information between them; it requires considerable social skills to win acceptance in the different groups, however.

Social entrepreneurs have another role, which involves acting independently of economic entrepreneurs, and even challenging their business methods. Social entrepreneurs can mount initiatives to address the consequences of economic failure. When a firm goes bankrupt, owing money to its suppliers and employees, then workers may be forced into unemployment and poverty, and its suppliers may fail as well. When a bankrupt firm is a dominant local employer, workers may have to leave the area to find work. Unemployment may lead to gambling, alcohol abuse and domestic violence. Society therefore needs to find a safety-net for people affected by business failure, and in the absence of state intervention this is provided by social entrepreneurs.

Social entrepreneurs can also challenge successful firms over wage rates, working conditions, pensions and job security, for example, by forming trades unions. They may also challenge the way products are marketed (e.g. alcohol and cigarettes targeted at young people), or argue that they should not be produced at all (e.g. prostitution).

Economic entrepreneurs therefore have an ambivalent relation with social entrepreneurs. Clubs and societies established by social entrepreneurs are useful to economic entrepreneurs in making contact with potential workers, customers and investors. On the other hand, some social entrepreneurs are perceived as trouble makers. The result is a political polarisation of clubs and societies: some are pro-business (for example, free-market (right-wing) political parties) some anti-business (for example trades unions, consumer groups, environmental groups) and others broadly neutral (for example sports clubs and enthusiasts' groups).

While social entrepreneurs can repair defects in the economy by facilitating contacts and building trust, economic entrepreneurs have limited ability to repair defects in society. Because business behaviour is embedded in social structures, social failure ultimately leads to business failure. If society fragments and respect for the rule of law breaks down then business simply cannot function properly. Thus social entrepreneurship is necessary for business entrepreneurship, but the converse does not apply.

Business contributes indirectly to society by providing a range of products that facilitate social networking. Technological innovations

DOI: 10.1057/9781137305824

made by economic entrepreneurs have facilitated long-distance social networking by promoting remote communication (e.g. postal systems, telephones and the internet) and long-distance travel (e.g. railways, jet airliners). On the other hand, innovations such as television and video games may have discouraged social networking, as critics have pointed out.

5.4 The impact of economic and social entrepreneurship on the evolution of the economy, 1200–2000

It is instructive to compare the interplay of economic and social entrepreneurship at the beginning and end of the period of study. The exercise reveals that changes in business enterprise, government, religion and society have been inextricably linked. It suggests that while entrepreneurship has not fundamentally changed over the period, attitudes to entrepreneurship have shifted quite considerably. It might be expected that modern attitudes to entrepreneurship would be more enlightened than medieval attitudes, but careful consideration, in the light of the preceding analysis, suggests that the opposite may be true.

In 1200 government was in the hands of dynastic monarchy, and monarchs perceived their primary role to be that of warrior. They defended the country's borders, maintained law and order, and acquired additional territories by aggression when circumstances permitted. They relied on the goodwill of local warlords (barons), but also needed to assert authority over them. There was no welfare state. Taxes were collected, as and when required, to pay for wars and for the expenses of the royal court, but not for poor relief. Poor relief was mainly the responsibility of well-to-do citizens, as explained below.

The English tax system was efficient by the standards of the time. Building on the foundations of Anglo-Saxon administration, William the Conqueror compiled the Domesday books to assess the country's taxable assets. But there was no personal income tax, as noted earlier. This meant that the monarchy was always interested in revenue-raising schemes such as chartering markets, monopolising the wool trade, collecting duties on imported luxuries, and so on. The Norman state was, on balance, more of a business enterprise dedicated to financing war than it was an under-developed welfare state.

DOI: 10.1057/9781137305824

The church was dedicated to funding prayer and worship of the highest possible standard. Religion was a papal monopoly, run very much along business lines, as explained in Chapter 4. Funds were raised from royal patronage, private endowments (e.g. gifts of land to support chantries), and the pilgrim trade. Some monastic orders, such as the Franciscans, ministered to the poor, but Christian good works were, on the whole, the responsibility of the devout laity. Apart from almshouses and hospitals, there was little organised charity.

With neither church nor state providing much organised welfare, family members were an important source of support. An implicit inter-generational contract obliged parents to provide education and training for sons (and arranged marriages for daughters) who would then provide for them in their old age. In the absence of universal schooling, many children followed their parents into the same trade. Where the parent was self-employed, this encouraged the development of a dynastic family business.

Community was also important. While goods were traded over long distances, people often stayed put, and this encouraged local ties. The growth of towns stimulated the growth of guilds. Some were purely social fraternities, or were dedicated to the upkeep of facilities, such as a bridge or chapel. Others were associated with a particular trade or profession; some were for artisans (who often lived in a special part of the town dedicated to their trade) and others for merchants. Merchant guilds helped members to transport their goods safely in convoys, to invest in each other businesses, and to marry into each other's families.

Entrepreneurship was important to all sectors of society. Business activities funded both church and state. Artisans ran family businesses in the towns, as did farmers in the countryside. Merchants sometimes sent their younger relatives abroad to act as their agents in foreign ports. Even itinerants, such as peddlers and hawkers, could be regarded as low-level entrepreneurs.

By 2000 government religion and society had changed quite considerably, but entrepreneurship had not. Commodities were more varied and technologically more sophisticated, but small family businesses were still in evidence, alongside larger firms. The main difference lay in the presence of these larger firms, and in the individualistic values espoused by their leaders.

The warrior culture of the monarchy had largely disappeared, and a democratic welfare state had taken its place. Citizens enjoyed free healthcare and education, a state pension and there were benefits for the disabled and unemployed. This was funded mainly from a progressive income tax levied on individuals, together with a value added tax. Due to privatisation in the 1990s, government no longer controlled energy and transport utilities, coal mines or steel plants. The re-distribution of income remained a key role throughout the post-war period, however.

Organised religion remained important but there was also considerable apathy and downright scepticism regarding religion too. But although religious observance had declined, charity was well-organised and charitable giving was substantial. Guilds were almost extinct (London livery companies excepted), but there were many clubs, societies, professional associations, trade associations, and so on.

Banking and financial arrangements had become much more sophisticated. The creation of the national debt, and a substantial growth in the number and size of joint-stock companies, made available a wide range of financial assets for investment purposes. These could be packaged into unit trusts or used as an asset base by pension funds; the income from such funds could provide a convenient pension plan. Many professionals enjoyed access to a generous occupational pension.

The emergence of large joint-stock companies created a potential divorce between ownership and control, in which the owners of the firm (the shareholders) lost effective control of the managers (who were mainly salaried employees). In the corporate society of the 1950s and 1960s, many managers of large firms committed themselves to a high-wage policy, and with slow productivity growth which made firms increasingly uncompetitive and eroded profits. The response was to advocate shareholder capitalism in which managers were expected to put profit ahead of every other consideration, such as workers' welfare. Charitable objectives, it was said, were not appropriate for firms, but only for individuals.

The failure of many large firms opened up opportunities for small firms, many of them established by experienced managers made redundant by large firms. Governments encouraged this move, as the new firm founders created jobs for themselves as well as their employees, and thereby reduced unemployment and hence benefit claims. Governments encouraged the development of an enterprise culture in which small-firm founders acquired an heroic status.

These small firms were somewhat different from the small firms of the medieval period, however, because they were not so closely based

DOI: 10.1057/9781137305824

upon family ties. The objective was not to create a dynastic business for the benefit of future generations, but a business for the benefit of the entrepreneur themselves. The family no longer had the same economic importance as it did in the medieval period. The growth of the welfare state, the presence of organised charities, and the development of pensions meant that the family was deemed unnecessary as a means of support in old age.

As a result, small-firm entrepreneurs increasingly took their cue from large firms. They dedicated themselves to maximising shareholder value, with the added twist that as the principal shareholder they would get all the profit. Unlike traditional businesses, there was no family obligation to constrain them, and often no religious scruples either. Small business became just as 'lean and mean' as big business.

Transport and communication was more advanced in 2000 and, as a result, markets were wider and mobility greater. The differences should not be exaggerated, however. International trade in the thirteenth century was promoted by advances in ship design and the improvement of ports. Long-distance trade is still conducted mainly by sea today, but the ships are much larger, somewhat faster, and less dependent on the wind. Similarly sun-seeking tourists heading for the continent in 2000 were not that different from the pilgrims of the middle ages, although there were more of them, and their journeys were quicker and cheaper.

The main differences relate to inland movements, where roads have drastically improved due to better drainage, metalled surfaces and motor vehicles. People now travel further to do their shopping, leading to a decline in the number of market centres compared to the middle ages. London has consistently grown faster than other English cities, transforming some provincial centres into a London 'back office' location. Labour mobility has substantially increased, weakening ties with families and local communities.

Communication technology has dramatically advanced as well. As robots have taken over production activities, work has been re-located from the shop floor to the office. The internet has dramatically speeded up remote communication, and has begun to compensate for weaker ties with families and local communities by generating virtual relationships to replace them. These new ties are often based on shared interests, schooling and professional background rather than family or locality. Since 2000 this trend has accelerated, with increasing number of people socialising on the internet rather than face-to face.

DOI: 10.1057/9781137305824

Advances in transport and communication have provided new opportunities for entrepreneurs. Some involve the development of new technology, such as CCTV surveillance, whilst others exploit the technology that is already developed, for example, interactive online games. Others arise because new infrastructure has reduced transport and communication costs and encouraged the development and marketing of truly global products. Large firms often provide a route to market for small firms developing new products that the large firms add to their product portfolios. Small firms can also participate in global supply chains as associate producers, wholesalers, retailers and franchisees.

Large firms are typically funded by a host of separate investors, few of whom take any active interest in the company. The few investors that take an interest tend to be large financial institutions, such as pension funds, who are simply interested in profit income. Any entrepreneur who transforms their business into a listed company by a public issue of shares is liable to find that effective control has fallen into the hands of a financial institution, or a group of such institutions. If these institutions judge that the entrepreneur is failing to maximise profit then the entrepreneur will be displaced from their executive role. There is no longer any place for loyalty to customers, workers or suppliers, or preservation of family traditions, unless these can be shown to directly increase profit.

Large firms managed under these constraints cannot respond to social problems, for example, by maintaining employment in a recession. Sacking the workers and re-engaging them when required is the only policy acceptable to absentee owners interested solely in profit. If there are social problems then it is the responsibility of private individuals to intervene. There is no obligation on the firm that causes the social problems to do anything about it because their duty is to the shareholders alone, and they are unlikely to be aware of any problems the firm is creating because they take no interest in it anyway.

This is a marked contrast to the situation in the middle ages, when many of the large employers were social, religious or political institutions. These institutions had recognised obligations, which constrained the methods that they used to obtain their income. Like the modern corporation, they needed profits to survive, but unlike the modern corporation they could trade these profits off against the social costs incurred in making them. If they failed to make this trade off then they would lose legitimacy, and this might ultimately undermine their authority.

DOI: 10.1057/9781137305824

Enterprise culture in 2000 asserted that maximising profit was justification enough for any business method. It was becoming clear, however, that many consumers disagreed. Social entrepreneurs created movements designed to monitor working conditions in global supply chains, and elsewhere. They argued that profits should not be made from child-labour or from workers paid less than the subsistence wage. Impacts on the environment, human health, and animal welfare also became popular concerns through the efforts of other social entrepreneurs.

Social entrepreneurs turned the power of the brand against the firms that owned the brands, by threatening to tarnish their brands. They believed, correctly it would seem, that the public would be shocked if they knew what really lay behind the wholesome image of some of the products that they regularly purchased. There is little evidence that these social entrepreneurs were seeking to make profits for themselves; if they were then they would almost certainly have blackmailed the firms they had evidence against and the public would not have got to hear about the problem.

5.5   Conclusions

This book has set out a new research agenda: to create a systematic history of entrepreneurship. The agenda is interdisciplinary because it involves building bridges between entrepreneurship studies and business history. Indeed, the range of relevant disciplines is very wide, because entrepreneurship studies are informed by economics and management studies, while business history is related to other branches of history – social and cultural, economic and political.

Chapter 2 surveyed the modern economic theory of entrepreneur-ship, and argued that it is both rigorous and robust, and therefore provides a good foundation for historical work. Chapter 3 applied the theory to innovation in the English economy, 1200–2000. The analysis distinguished different types of innovation – notably technological and institutional – and argued that institutional innovation is of greater importance than usually appreciated. Following Schumpeter, it argued that innovations often occur in waves, and that these waves account for some of the 'revolutions' that historians have detected. Although the dating of revolutions is tricky, and the attribution of innovations controversial, the results of the exercise are sufficiently promising to be explored in more detail in future work.

DOI: 10.1057/9781137305824

Chapter 4 presented a series of case studies based on the secondary literature, with an emphasis on the medieval period. These studies reveal some of the links between entrepreneurs and the businesses they establish, and show that context is critically important to the way that a business evolves. Fortunately, the theory of entrepreneurship is sufficiently general that it encompasses these contexts, and thereby facilitates the interpretation of the case studies.

This chapter has examined the social and institutional aspects of entrepreneurship and illustrated how deeply business is embedded in society. It has argued that an ideology based on the pursuit of profit in a perfectly functioning market economy is inappropriate for regulating an entrepreneurial economy. In an economy where information is widely distributed and seriously incomplete, entrepreneurs will always make mistakes, and these mistakes will have adverse consequences. In many cases entrepreneurs can walk away from the problems they create because they have already wasted all the resources that might have been used to put things right. Social entrepreneurs therefore need to step in to clear things up.

Social entrepreneurs also have a role in preventing or mitigating problems before they occur. When the business sector is dominated by family enterprises, families can impose their own value systems on the way their businesses are run, but when firms are owned by absentee shareholders it is likely that the only value system will be the maximisation of profit. In this case social entrepreneurs can influence profit calculations by policing the integrity of corporate brands. This aligns profit more closely with public concerns, and reinstates some of the restraints on socially irresponsible entrepreneurship that existed in the medieval economy.

Further reading

For the role of social entrepreneurship in engineering trust, and its relation to conventional entrepreneurship, see

Casson, M. (2010) *Entrepreneurship: Theory, Networks, History* (Cheltenham: Edward Elgar).

An entertaining overview of social networks and inter-personal connectivity is provided in

Watts, D. J. (2004) *Six Degrees: The Science of a Connected Age* (London: Vintage).

DOI: 10.1057/9781137305824

For historical studies of social networks that support, and in some cases constrain, entrepreneurship see

Gestrich, A. and M. Schulte-Beerbuhl (eds) (2011) *Cosmopolitan Networks in Commerce and Society, 1660–1914* (London: German Historical Institute).

Haggerty, S. (2006) *The British-Atlantic Trading Community, 1760–1810: Men, Women and the Distribution of Goods* (Leiden: E. J. Brill).

Mackenney, R. (1987) *Tradesmen and Traders: The World of the Guilds in Venice and Europe, c.1250–c.1650* (Totowa, NJ: Banes & Noble).

Murdoch, S. (2006) *Network North; Scottish Kin, Commercial and Covert Association in Northern Europe, 1603–1746* (Leiden: E. J. Brill).

Wilson, J. F. and A. Popp (eds) (1994) *Industrial Clusters and Regional Business Networks in England, 1750–1950* (Aldershot: Ashgate).

For a definitive study of English chambers of commerce and a review of English trade associations see

Bennett, R. J. (2011) *Local Business Voice* (Oxford: Oxford University Press).

Political and Economic Planning (1957) *Industrial Trade Associations: Activities and Organisation* (London: PEP).

DOI: 10.1057/9781137305824

Index

DOI: 10.1057/9781137305824

DOI: 10.1057/9781137305824

DOI: 10.1057/9781137305824

DOI: 10.1057/9781137305824

Lightning Source UK Ltd.
Milton Keynes UK
UKOW040156220613

212649UK00002B/11/P